ENDORSEMENTS

"I've always appreciated how Bryan can communicate complicated ideas and concepts very simply and clearly. His book, *Worthy of the Gift*, is a perfect example. Bryan weaves in best practices of financial stewardship for organizations in a very relatable story. I highly recommend this excellent book!"

—Lloyd Kim, Coordinator, Mission to the World

"Every ministry and nonprofit strives to share its vision and raise funds. This book does an incredible job of taking these complicated tasks and using storytelling to help us understand the concepts, followed by practical step-by-step guidance on how to implement them in our own organizations. Bryan's decades of partnering with organizations make him uniquely qualified to take us on this beautiful journey. This book should become required reading for all current and future ministry leaders!"

—Mark A. Robison, CPCU, Chairman & President, Brotherhood Mutual

"This is an enjoyable read that communicates fundraising best practices in a practical way. You don't need to apply every principle, but you are sure to gain a new insight or be reminded of the importance of something you may want to improve."

—Vonna Laue, Executive Director of Global Services/CFO, TEAM

"This book is a much-needed resource for Kingdom-minded organizations. The practical application demonstrated through an engaging Fable is sure to make this a well-read book. Organizations that follow this guidance will be well served!"

—Fran Brown, Partner-In-Charge, CapinCrouse

"Trust. It takes years to build but is quickly lost. Bryan has done a masterful job in capturing our minds and imagination in becoming an organization that is truly worthy of the gift. You won't want to put this book down as Bryan equips us to become "'A steward of stewards'."

—Jake Lapp, Vice President of Member Accountability, ECFA

"Bryan Taylor masterfully utilizes the power of storytelling to help us experience what he describes as the *worthiness continuum*. You'll gather lessons learned along the way and discover the ultimate reward of faithful stewardship. Understanding and inspiring generosity is a spiritual journey, and this one touches on every stakeholder associated with a Christ-centered nonprofit. I encourage nonprofit leaders at every level to read this book and assess their progress toward becoming *worthy of every gift* they receive."

—Tami Heim, President & CEO, Christian Leadership Alliance

"In an age of deep skepticism and self-preservation, Bryan Taylor casts a bigger vision—one where generosity becomes a meaningful act of trust, purpose, and cultural renewal. *Worthy of the Gift* equips leaders to build authentic relationships with donors by living and leading with integrity. It's a timely blueprint for those who want to steward wealth and mission with wisdom."

—Gabe Lyons, President, THINQ_Media & Author

"*Worthy of the Gift* is a powerful reminder that faithful stewardship begins not with strategy, but with reverence—and Bryan Taylor is a guide you can trust."

—Jake Bland, President, Youth For Christ

"A powerful teaching tool for leaders, pastors, and anyone seeking to live with purpose, written by someone whom I highly respect. Highly recommend!"

—Bryan Clontz, Ph.D., CFP, CAP,
President, Charitable Solutions, LLC

"Great insights are often drawn by men and women who have spent meaningful time in the arena," and are willing to share their hard-fought learnings with others in the spirit of making a broader movement better. This book is just that—highly recommend."

—Luke Roush, Co-Founder & Co-CEO,
Sovereign's Capital

"*Worthy of the Gift* offers wisdom and inspiration to move your donor relationships from transactional to transformational. Strategic guidance is provided with clarity and conviction. Your team will be able to align organizational vision with your donors' passion for funding long-term impact. Appealing to both thought and heart, Bryan Taylor brings spiritual depth and actionable counsel to move fundraising to the next level. This work is an essential resource that will enhance your worthiness to secure transformational gifts!"

—Phil Purcell, MPA/JD

"For years, I have learned from and trusted Bryan Taylor. God has blessed him with extraordinary gifts, a knack for teaching, and real-world experience, making him a close advisor to me and many other nonprofit leaders. His book is not about fundraising razzle-dazzle; it's about the lasting structures and time-tested practices that transform a vision into a force for good. It will help you build, grow, and lead an exceptional organization that donors will find deeply satisfying to support over and over again."

—Eric Fleshood, Chief Executive Officer, Cru Foundation

"I've known and worked with Bryan Taylor for almost 30 years. He has the expertise to explain how an organization can become worthy of transformational gifts. Gifts that are not only transformational for an organization but also transformational for the donor. I have had the privilege of personally seeing the impact when organizations seek to cultivate a worthiness culture."

—Bruce Owens, Consultant, Lifestyle Giving

Note: Those who provided the reviews, endorsements, or recommendations printed herein, of *Worthy of the Gift: A Fable* or its author, received no cash or non-cash compensation from the publisher, the author, or from Cornerstone Management, Inc. for their participation.

WORTHY OF THE GIFT

A FABLE

By

BRYAN TAYLOR

Published by Leadership Books, Inc., Las Vegas, NV – New York, NY

LeadershipBooks.com

ISBN
Hardback: 978-1-971546-06-3
Paperback: 978-1-971546-07-0
eBook: 978-1-971546-08-7

Leadership Books, Inc. is committed to publishing works of quality and integrity. In that spirit, we are proud to offer this book to our readers. This is a work of fiction. Unless otherwise indicated, all the names, characters, businesses, places, events, and incidents in this book are either the product of the Author's imagination or used in a fictitious manner. Any resemblance to actual persons, living or dead, or actual events is purely coincidental.

General Disclosures / Disclaimers

The opinions expressed herein are those of Bryan Taylor as of the date of publication and are subject to change without notice. While the publisher and author have used their best efforts in preparing this book, they make no representations or warranties with respect to the accuracy or completeness of the contents of this book. This material is for informational use only and is not intended as an offer or solicitation with respect to the purchase or sale of any security or for the services of

LEADERSHIP
Thoughtful, Relevant Leaders From Around The World
BOOKS

DEDICATION

For my Mom, who did so much to inspire my joy for reading.
I wish you were here to read and celebrate with me.

TABLE OF CONTENTS

ACKNOWLEDGEMENTS

In many ways, writing a book is a communal effort! Countless people have supported, encouraged, and guided me along the way as I have worked to complete this book. I want to take the opportunity to express my appreciation to all those who have been a part of this project. While it would be impossible for me to thank each of you personally, please know that I am indebted to you because, without you, this book would not have been completed.

In that spirit, there are those who deserve special recognition for the significant role they played in the completion of this project. I owe a particular debt of gratitude to my wife Christy, not only for her unfailing love, but also for her unflagging belief in my ability to write. To my four children: Brent, Cole, Ann, and Clay! Thank you for your patience with my late nights, writing trips, and the anxiety that accompanies any significant endeavor. I am extremely grateful for each of you, and your faith in my ability to complete this project has been more encouraging than you will ever know. I would not be the person I am today without your love and engagement!

Thank you to my team at Cornerstone, and particularly to my partners: Tamara, Winters, and Chad. I deeply appreciate your understanding and patience as I sought to complete this project in the midst of an already-busy season. Without your encouragement, support, and covering, I would not have been able to dedicate the time or resources to finish the book. You, along with our entire team, have proofread, offered ideas, and critiqued my thought process all along the way—and I have no doubt the book is better because of your involvement.

Special thanks to Karen Sillay! Karen, without you, I would never have been able to find the time to write a book, or pushed through in some of the more difficult periods of the process. Your willingness to help me set aside time, track updates, and work on the project along with me has been invaluable.

I'm particularly grateful for the love and support of my broader family. Dad, without your leadership, belief in me, and constant prayer support, I would not be where I am today, and I certainly would not have been able to complete this book. Patty, Eric, and Mary Ruth, thank you for your belief in me and your desire to support my writing efforts.

Thanks to my daughter-in-law, Nicole, for her willingness to read an early version of the Fable and provide candid feedback! Your willingness to take time to read through the material on short notice was deeply appreciated.

Over the last 25 years, many ministries and ministry leaders have contributed to the formation of the Worthy of the Gift conceptual framework. Ray Lyne, Bruce Owens, Jerry Wear, Paul Kooistra, and many others have taught and modeled these concepts. The many institutional and individual clients I have had the privilege to serve have all played a part in the development of this framework and the Fable that accompanies it. Your heart for the Kingdom and for your donors has inspired me through the years and provided the real-life lessons that lie behind both the Fable and the Worthy of the Gift Continuum itself. Thank you for your faithfulness and stewardship.

Finally, I want to acknowledge the many professional associates who have supported me in various ways as I have worked on this project. Many of you offered counsel, real-life experiences, and personal as well as professional support while I worked on this project. Special thanks to the team at Hixon Zuercher Capital Management, and Tony Hixon in particular, for his steadfast encouragement as I sought to finish the book.

FOREWORD

There's a scene in Acts that grips me—in the best way. Ananias brings an offering to God, pretending it's everything, but secretly holds some back. What happens next reminds us: God doesn't just see the gift: *He sees the heart behind it.*

That's what I kept thinking about as I read *Worthy of the Gift.*

Not because it's a book about fundraising. But because it's a book about being a worthy steward.

Over the years, I've sat in countless rooms like the ones Bryan Taylor describes—boardrooms, budget meetings, and donor dinners—and from time to time, Bryan was right there with me. Some of the best lessons I've learned came from those moments, usually over breakfast or coffee.

What's on these pages isn't just theory. It's truth forged through decades of experience and wisdom, and you can trust the man who wrote it. Bryan has walked alongside Youth For Christ's Foundation for well over a decade, offering the kind of perspective and challenge that have shaped our culture of stewardship.

When I first started journeying with Bryan, the YFC Foundation was in its earliest and most humble days. We were dreaming big but had very little to show for it. Over time, and by God's grace, we've seen the resources entrusted to us by faithful donors grow more than thirtyfold. Through it all, Bryan has remained a trusted voice. Many times, I've walked away from a conversation with him not just encouraged, but more aligned with the heart of God for our mission. And I'm convinced that we're still only just getting started.

Even though this book is written as a story, it's packed with tangible, actionable steps. If followed, they will sharpen your culture and strengthen your stewardship in ways that could truly make your ministry *worthy of the gift.*

Our team has leaned into this material significantly over the years. Not just because it's helpful, but because it parallels the way we've come to think about building long-term relationships with our donors. It's not about gimmicks. It's about godliness. It's not about impressing people. It's about being found faithful.

This fable is a holy gutcheck. Not just for fundraisers, but for every ministry leader who has ever received a sacrificial gift in Jesus' name. It dares to ask, not, "How do we get more?" but "Are we truly worthy of what we've already received?"

That question is not about performance. It's about posture.

This book reminds us that donors aren't giving to a spreadsheet. They're giving to a Kingdom vision. They're entrusting us with worship: acts of faith, not transactions. That should cause us to tremble.

It also shows us why policies matter. Financial controls matter. Board structure matters. But only when they reflect something deeper: that the God we serve is holy, and He deserves more than efficiency. He deserves reverence.

Bryan's characters, Jim, Koen, Tom, and Doug, don't just build an organization. They build a culture. One that says, "We will be found faithful." And that's what I long for in our generation of ministry leaders: not just vision, but holiness. Not just energy, but integrity. Not just results, but repentance when needed.

So if you're a CEO, a board member, a development officer, a pastor, or just someone with a growing sense that God has entrusted you with something sacred, I invite you to read slowly. Let this story do its work.

Let it make you uncomfortable. Let it stir a new commitment to be the kind of leader and to build the kind of ministry that is truly worthy of the gift.

Because the gifts we've been entrusted with were never ours to begin with.

They belong to Jesus.

And He is worthy of it all.

—Jake Bland, CEO,
Youth For Christ USA & YFC Foundation

PART ONE

THE FABLE

CELEBRATION

Jim Anderson gazed at the sunlight dancing on the water. It was a beautiful morning in the mountains of Colorado, and the early morning breeze ruffled the water of the resort's pristine lake. The waves, barely more than ripples, really, lapped quietly at the stony beach. An eagle soared overhead, effortlessly riding the mountain thermals. He had come a long way over the last 20 years, and so had Chrysalis. *Was it possible*, he wondered, *was Chrysalis really on the verge of achieving those goals he and Koen had set so many years ago?*

As he admired the view, Jim's mind drifted back in time to another morning long ago.

THE CHALLENGE (25 YEARS AGO)

A cold wind drove the rain against the window, and the slate-grey sky appeared dim and unyielding. Jim clutched his cup of coffee and tried to shrug off the dreariness and cold of the day. He really shouldn't be standing here at the window, he thought. He had a million things to do today: donors to call, a meeting to discuss the new endowed chair for philosophy, and his high-school daughter's soccer game later that afternoon. Instead, he stood looking out the window and took another sip of coffee.

His phone buzzed, and the voice of Holly, his administrative assistant, came through the intercom, "Jim, I have Dr. Koen Ridder on line one."

That's odd, Jim thought. *What was Dr. Ridder calling him about at this time in the morning on Monday?*

"Thanks, Holly," Jim said, "go ahead and put him through."

"Will do," Holly answered, and a moment later the phone rang again. Jim picked it up and heard Koen Ridder's voice on the other end of the line.

"Morning, Koen," he said, "what can I do for you?" "Well, Jim, I've got a problem," Koen said. Koen had recently left the college where Jim worked to take the president's position at a small, faith-based, global, non-governmental organization (NGO). Jim didn't know too much about the situation, but he had the highest regard for Dr. Ridder. Koen had almost singlehandedly turned the college around and put it on a firm financial footing. Jim had been finishing up a graduate degree when Dr. Ridder picked up on his background in sales and asked him to consider a development role at the college. That was three years ago, and the college had since made tremendous strides – in no small part due to Jim's efforts along with Dr. Ridder and other members of the advancement team.

Koen paused, then launched into the conversation. "The thing is, Jim, the situation here is bad. The organization has landed in some real trouble, and I have my work cut out for me. We are swimming in red ink over here, and getting ourselves out of this ditch will take significant work. I can't do it alone, Jim. I need help, and I believe you are just the man for the job!"

Jim was stunned; he had no plans to leave Seattle.

Things at the college had started humming along well, with a growing endowment and stable enrollment. They had even kicked off a new building campaign. "Uh, Koen, I don't know what to say." Jim managed to stutter through the mouthpiece.

"Well," Koen boomed, "just say yes! I've got the perfect position for you here, Jim. I want to make you my new VP for Development! You'll report directly to me, and only to me. Jim, I've got to get this ship righted, and to do that, I need you. I watched you at the college. You were my most effective development officer. You figured out what we needed to do, and you were not afraid to do it! You stepped up, Jim, and together we raised a lot of money that changed the lives of students! This is a special opportunity to impact the lives of thousands of hurting people, Jim. I think we can apply what you've learned, and together we can stabilize this organization. Not only that, but I believe we can also prepare the organization for tremendous impact as we enter the new millennium, offering the hope of Christ to hundreds of thousands, perhaps millions of hurting people displaced by armed conflict around the world. What do you say, Jim? Are you with me?"

Jim's mind spun a mile a minute. *This was crazy! What would Ann say, and what about the girls? Missy was just getting settled, and Abby loved her new club soccer team.*

Could he really take them all the way across the country to start a new life in Greenville?

"I, I don't know," Jim said haltingly. "This is a really big step, I mean, to leave the college, and the Northwest, to move back to the South? I'm really not sure what to say at this moment, Koen."

"Well," Koen said, "pray about it! Talk to Ann. I've really got to have you, Jim! I can't do this on my own, and I know you're the right man for the job. Together, we can turn this place around! I've got plans, Jim, and Chrysalis has a special vision. It's not every day you get to provide hope to people displaced by conflict and struggling just to survive. We're offering them a new start, Jim. Hope for the future, and it all begins with Jesus. Jim, God can use you here, and I need you. Together, I know we can make a difference."

Jim knew that was true. If there was one thing he could count on, it was that Koen would have his back and support him all the way. After all, it was Koen who had spotted him for this development role in the first place. As a financial planner and insurance salesman, Jim was settled into a good gig, he thought. But Koen had convinced him that his real calling was in fundraising. Even while finishing up grad school, he left a promising career in corporate America and jumped into his role at the college with both feet. He never looked back.

Together, he and Koen had rebuilt the general fund and even started adding to the college's small endowment. In just a few years, he saw more impact than he ever expected, and along the way, he learned a thing or two as well. *To take that knowledge and have the free rein to apply it fully would be an exciting new adventure,* he thought, *but Greenville? Really? What would Ann say?*

"Ok, Koen," he said. "I'll give it some thought. I'll pray about it, and I'll talk to Ann."

"Great!" Koen's loud voice shouted through the phone. "But don't take too long, Jim! Like I said, we've got a lot of making up to do over here, and I need you right away. I can give you a couple of weeks to make up your mind, but then I really want you here in Greenville!"

CELEBRATION

From his perch on the veranda, Jim reflected, *that was how it all began, nearly 25 years ago now*. Hard to believe how long ago he, Ann, and the girls had picked up all they owned and headed to Greenville to begin a new life and a new job at Chrysalis.

"Jim," Ann called from inside the hotel suite. "What time is the first event?"

"Breakfast is at 8:30 and the opening remarks from Koen are at 9:30," Jim replied.

This was the tenth President's Weekend that Chrysalis had hosted. In the rearview mirror, Jim could see 25 years of planning and 25 years of work. Were they going to make it? Had they really moved far enough along the **worthiness continuum** to achieve their goals? *It just doesn't seem possible,* Jim thought.

When Jim joined Koen at Chrysalis, they hammered out a plan over the first year of his tenure–not only to fund Chrysalis's current budget, but also to expand the vision, offset administrative expenses for field personnel, and buffer monthly cash flow.

As he headed inside for a shower, Jim reflected on those early days at Chrysalis.

WORTHINESS (20 YEARS AGO)

"Things are getting better," Tom said, "but not nearly where they should be!" Tall, professorial, and ascetic, Tom was Chrysalis's CFO. Like Jim, Tom was recruited by Koen to help turn Chrysalis around. He and Jim discussed the organization over coffee at a small diner in downtown Greenville.

"Koen has done a great job getting out and talking to donors," Tom said, "and they're listening. After all, he's a great vision caster and the whole Chrysalis team is now pulling in the same direction because of his efforts."

Koen spent his first couple of years at Chrysalis "getting things in order" as he called it. After hiring Jim, they began engaging current Chrysalis donors. Koen communicated with passion; a significant part of his role centered around fundraising. As President of the organization, he felt that for Chrysalis to be **worthy** of the gifts they received, they must communicate the vision and mission with utmost clarity!

An impressive leader, Koen's persona came across as confident and determined! The tall and lanky Dr. Koen Ridder exuded determination to turn Chrysalis around.

When the board first recruited him to the organization, they had a small, core group of donors, a solid field staff, and a 30-year history of mixed results. Under previous leadership, Chrysalis had lost its way and floundered to recover. With giving, ministry impact, and morale heading in the wrong direction, the board began looking for a turnaround specialist. They saw the skill with which Koen had turned things around at Spruce Mountain College (SMC) in Seattle. He offered them the hope of a better future than the one implied by their current trajectory.

Not one to waste time, Koen quickly assessed the situation. Combining vision casting with accountability and donor centricity, he described the new approach as a quest for worthiness. Under his leadership, they expanded their understanding of worthiness beyond faithfulness and dependability to include aspects like perseverance, clarity, and meticulous stewardship. Koen challenged his team to a higher standard.

Chrysalis enjoyed a unique donor base. As a mission-sending organization, the missionary field staff raised their own support through a deputized fundraising model. A portion of that missional support went to cover the organization's administrative expenses, but Chrysalis also enjoyed the capacity to raise corporate funds to support the vision and mission of Chrysalis further. Upon coming to Chrysalis, Koen quickly realized the organization had a **worthy** vision and mission but struggled to secure funding. Their current approach had little chance of receiving a transformational gift because of problems with donor communication and accountability. He knew that if he wanted to improve funding and inspire donors, Chrysalis would need to be **Worthy of the Gift**.

In reviewing the organization's financial statements, it became quite obvious that they had allowed expenses to drift higher, putting pressure on the administrative draw from Chrysalis's missionaries. Furthermore, less-than-successful direct fundraising resulted in a diminishing general fund, leaving the ministry to sustain itself on historic reserves. Clearly, the situation needed to change!

Koen's first official action as President was to replace the CFO. He restructured the finance department and brought in Thomas Rowling. Tom's co-workers knew him to be "tough but fair." His level, gray eyes, set in a weathered face, peered out from horned rim spectacles.

Only the rare individual could match Tom's capacity for numbers. His mind seemed to be a virtual calculator, and he never forgot anything. In his usual way, Koen brought Tom in and turned him loose.

"The situation's a shambles, Tom!" Koen exclaimed, "We have some great people, but we lack leadership, and funding is drying up. We spent a fortune on corporate travel last year alone. We must do something, Tom, and I've no doubt you're just the man to do it. Let me know what you need!" Off he went, but that was Koen.

Tom came in and went to work. He quickly and pleasantly surmised that Chrysalis had a solid finance team. They had, as Koen said, simply lacked good leadership. His senior controller, Elizabeth Jones, was "as good as they come," but, like many controllers, she stayed head down in the details. The well-kept, detailed, and complete corporate financials told Tom his hunch was right: the problem lay with decisions at the top.

Tom invited Elizabeth into his office to review the situation. In her mid-50s and graying a bit at her temples, she gave it to him straight. With a twinkle in her green eyes, she shared her passion for the organization, but also her frustration with current practices. Her clear and direct, clipped northern accent let him know that Chrysalis hadn't undergone an audit in several years, and while she had done her best to keep the accounting team going, she had little control over large expenses in the last few years. *That would have to change,* Tom thought.

"Anything else?" he asked.

"Well," Elizabeth hesitated, "honestly, I'm concerned about the future of Chrysalis. I love this organization, and I believe in our mission, but it's clear to me as I look at the finances that things are not going well. Since you've known Koen for quite a while, I just wondered what you think our chances are to, you know, turn things around?"

Tom took a moment to consider Elizabeth's question quietly. "Things are tough," Tom said thoughtfully, "and it will clearly take some work, and more importantly, some prayer to turn this ship around, but Koen is a man of action, and he has a plan. He's focused on improving the worthiness of Chrysalis."

"Worthiness?" Elizabeth asked. "What does that mean?"

"Well," Tom answered, "as I understand it. Worthiness begins with a **worthy** mission and vision."

"But we already have a vision," Elizabeth answered, confused.

"That's true," Tom answered, "but can you articulate that vision and mission clearly in 30 seconds or less?"

Elizabeth blushed, "Uh, well, we uh, send missionaries out to people...," her voice trailed off. "Maybe I know more about the numbers than what we are actually trying to do. I'm not quite as clear on that as I thought I was. I know we want to make a better world, something about transforming. Isn't that what a chrysalis does?" she stammered.

Tom chuckled, "That's okay, Elizabeth! You are not alone. But Koen's going to make sure we not only fully believe in our vision and mission, but also can articulate them fluently to anyone we meet. He calls it our 'elevator speech!'"

Tom smiled and continued, "We're all passionate about what we do, but we rarely think about the importance of clearly articulating our mission to those around us. At the end of the day, we are all representatives of Chrysalis.

"We need to convey our passion to everyone we meet. And that," Tom reflected, "would begin to turn the ship."

MISSION & VISION

A few days later, Koen held an all-hands meeting. The entire team at Chrysalis gathered in the meeting room and recorded the meeting to share with their missionaries on the field.

"Like many of you," Koen began, "I'm inspired by our vision here at Chrysalis! We exist to offer the hope of Jesus Christ to those displaced by armed conflict around the world! This is our vision! It is clear. It is compelling. And together we can bring it to fruition! As a team, we bring that vision into reality by living out our mission on a daily basis.

"Our mission is to provide food, shelter, and the message of Christ's love to human beings displaced by armed conflict around the globe. Many of you have heard me talk about **worthiness**. This is the first step in our journey along the **worthiness continuum**. We are a worthy organization because we have a vision and mission worthy of funding and support.

"Our ability to clearly communicate this vision and mission, coupled with our passion and belief in our mission, will empower us to connect with our donors and fund our efforts."

Koen looked out over the team. "Each one of you has a part to play in bringing this vision into reality. Each of us is an ambassador for Chrysalis! We must fully believe in the vision and the mission. And I have no doubt that each of you is passionate about our mission, or you wouldn't be sitting in this room today.

"However," Koen continued, "passion in and of itself is not enough. We must all be able to share this vision and mission fluently with anyone we meet. Make it your own! Write it and put it above your sink and recite it when you brush your teeth. It is not just my vision, or the board's vision; it is your vision! Practice with a co-worker, a spouse, or a friend, but clarify that vision and mission in your head. Let it get deep into your being! Be ready to share it at a moment's notice."

> Each member of the team must be able to communicate the vision in 30 seconds or less.

Koen picked up on the energy in the room. He saw everyone leaning in, engaged, and nodding in agreement. "As an organization, we change lives, and you are a vital part of that work. Your clarity of vision and focus on mission, no matter what your role, unites us as an organization and brings displaced and hurting people eternal hope. Ultimately, we want to share that vision with others so that they can be a part. We want to grow our donor base because that will lead to more changed lives. The first step in achieving that goal is for each of us to be able to communicate that vision in 30 seconds or less as we move forward along the **continuum of worthiness** and propel Chrysalis toward the fulfillment of this vision!"

CELEBRATION

The beauty of this morning seemed almost dazzling to Jim, or perhaps he was just excited! As his eyes followed the shadows of the billowing clouds and sun playing across the waves, Jim chuckled to himself as he thought back to Koen's speech so many years before.

The journey began with that speech! A journey, as Koen called it, along the **worthiness continuum**. A journey focused not only on returning Chrysalis to a solid financial footing, but also on preparing the organization to make that vision of changed lives a reality in the new millennium. As he dressed for the day, Jim reflected on the transformation within his team in the days following Koen's inspirational speech.

FINANCIAL ACCOUNTABILITY

So much change. Tom took the organization's financial situation in stride. Together with Elizabeth and the rest of the finance team, Tom started making changes in earnest.

He hired an audit firm and worked with Koen to set up a permanent finance and audit committee of the board. He set up an annual audit, worked cooperatively with the auditors, and reviewed the results with the committee. The committee would then make any necessary recommendations to the board.

Tom also decided that Chrysalis should apply for accreditation with ECFA. Founded in the 1970s, the Evangelical Council for Financial Accountability (ECFA) represented the gold standard among Christian organizations for transparency, stewardship, and financial accountability.

Tom recognized that every industry needed associations to help design best practices and provide accountability for their stakeholders. For Chrysalis, he knew that ECFA membership would help donors evaluate the financial health and stewardship of the organization.

Their membership would also demonstrate Chrysalis's desire to be a good steward of donor funds and faithfully apply those funds to fulfill the vision and mission of the organization. This step alone would go a long way toward building donor confidence and help to make the role of fundraisers—whether it was Koen and Jim, or the missionaries—that much easier.

Tom also worked hard with Elizabeth to create solid internal controls. He secured a solid banking relationship and began working with a bank to manage their cash reserves better and support the ongoing work of its field staff. Under the direction of Tom and Elizabeth, the finance team streamlined its financial procedures and partnered with the development department to creatively thank their donors as part of the receipting process.

At Spruce Mountain College (SMC), Jim and Koen had started raising funds to establish the college's endowment. Koen brought that vision with him to Chrysalis.

"What I want to do," he had told Jim, "is to build a 50-million-dollar endowment to help offset our administrative expenses and allow us to get missionaries to the field more easily!"

Fifty million! Jim thought, although he didn't say it out loud at the time. For a mission sending organization with an annual revenue of 15 million, this seemed almost impossible. Usually, mission sending organizations didn't even build endowments! Most aid organizations and mission sending agencies believed that building a large reserve or endowment would negatively impact giving and cause donors to believe the organization didn't need new donations.

But Koen had believed differently. After seeing the way that endowment was used to help fund programs and initiatives inside a collegiate institution, Koen believed he could apply that same mindset to Chrysalis. Further, he believed that Chrysalis must move *beyond cash* in its search for funding. In his work at SMC, Jim had helped convince Koen that donors held 90 percent of their wealth in noncash assets. For years, collegiate institutions had focused on a more comprehensive developmental approach to fundraising in addition to their student tuition. Together, Koen felt he and Jim would bring this approach to Chrysalis.

Koen and Jim agreed that Chrysalis needed a holistic approach to donor development. Koen had joked, "That's what I brought you here from Seattle to do, Jim! Show me the money!" Of course, Koen hadn't been serious. If anyone cared about Chrysalis donors more than Jim, it was Koen, who believed deeply in building meaningful relationships with donors. That was why he brought Jim on board. Jim cared about donors, and that's what Koen wanted for Chrysalis. He wanted a fundraising program that centered on the donor. Their donors' passion, vision, and Kingdom-impact ultimately mattered more than funding Chrysalis. If Chrysalis built a program around what served their donors best, Koen was convinced that Chrysalis's funding problems would be solved.

And so Jim had begun to do just that.

DONOR CENTRIC FUNDRAISING

At Spruce Mountain College, Jim had the opportunity to study and learn from new and cutting-edge programs in fundraising and development. Among those, he first learned about the difference between planned giving and current giving. Many, if not most, organizations focus almost exclusively on current giving: wanting to see a check in today's mail. In some ways, that is understandable. Every organization lives and dies by the need for current funding to maintain its mission. However, Jim believed it was shortsighted and, more importantly, it treated the donor like a vending machine.

Fundraising had become all about the transaction. In other words, "We have a worthy vision and mission and therefore you should 'fund' it." He noticed the transactional approach had become the basic mentality of most organizations he had evaluated. In fact, when he first started his role at SMC, Jim also saw himself as a hired gun, someone whose sole job was to "sell the donor" and emerge triumphantly from the engagement check in hand!

Jim's previous career in the insurance industry had prepared him well for this approach, as he developed a thick skin for rejection. His long-time fixation on distance running had also prepared him for the grueling perseverance necessary to close gifts. He did not fear rejection, and he had tenacity. Yes, Jim knew how to sell.

However, as he explored a variety of fundraising approaches employed by nonprofit organizations, Jim encountered a more holistic approach, more donor-centric in nature and focused on leveraging the donor's larger financial capacity.

Jim had introduced this approach at SMC, and it proved to be rather successful by both metrics of raising current dollars and also generating sizable gifts of assets. In fact, part of the reason Koen had reached out to Jim at SMC was because of his talent at building their donor development program. Koen believed Jim could do the same at Chrysalis.

Jim knew the importance of raising current funds to keep the ministry going while concurrently developing major donors and seeking larger transformational gifts to fund the endowment. While the two objectives seemed mutually exclusive to many, Jim felt confident that his more holistic, donor-centric model would work. After all, he had been trained by one of the best in the business!

While working at SMC and evaluating various fundraising models, Jim met a guru named Ray Lyne. By the time they'd met, Ray had been in the fundraising profession for nearly two decades and had pioneered a development model called "lifestyle giving." Ray's approach emphasized major donor development, and he believed in building a relationship with the donor by focusing on his or her calling as a *steward*. Ultimately, Ray taught, designing a framework that addressed the donor's long-term stewardship goals would result in the greatest potential for assets directed to charity, currently and in the future. This approach was about more than just the charity's needs or goals, and really sought to partner with donors by exploring their needs, desires, and expectations to form a mutually beneficial plan. Ultimately, Ray's model had been the catalyst for hundreds of millions of dollars flowing to Kingdom-oriented charities and nonprofits.

Jim believed that Ray's lifestyle giving approach fit well with Koen's philosophy of **worthiness**. An organization must be worthy of any gift, and part of that worthiness is related to the development office. In fact, Jim realized, the development office should actually function as the coach or trusted advisor to the donor in his or her stewardship calling and journey. To do this well at Chrysalis, Jim needed to be sure that the development and finance departments functioned well together as a team when it came to receiving gifts. Ultimately, Jim had to create a bridge between finance and development.

FINANCIAL BRIDGE

Under Koen's direction, Tom worked hard to put policies and procedures in place to offer greater transparency, accountability, and financial clarity. A focus on internal controls, the creation of the finance and audit committee, and ECFA membership had allowed Koen and Jim to begin rebuilding donor trust. Tom's focus on expense reduction and debt reduction began to pay off, and the organization slowly worked itself out of a rut. When Koen first came to Chrysalis, the organization was running in the red from a revenue perspective. Even more concerning, their total debt exceeded eight million dollars. Tom's skillful work, coupled with Koen and Jim's initial outreach to donors, had allowed the ministry to regain its financial footing.

As an extension of those initial efforts, Jim started working with Tom to create a "bridge" between finance and development. Jim remembered those early years when they couldn't afford extra help, so he and Tom had to work closely, as a team, to support donor engagement. While Jim and Koen spent a great deal of their time in the field calling on existing donors, they soon realized that would not be enough. They needed to broaden the base of donors and sharpen their clarity around the type of gifts they were willing to accept.

Tom, being Tom, of course, threw out a cautious complaint. "We can't just take any old asset! You all are going to saddle me with a useless piece of desert in Arizona! I'll never be able to sell it, and Chrysalis will be left paying taxes until Jesus comes back!

"Standards," Tom demanded, "we've got to have standards! I want to see this organization thrive just as much as the two of you, but there has to be some sort of guideline so we can know that the assets we accept will ultimately support our mission."

Jim could see the wisdom in Tom's comments and asked, "What if we create a gift acceptance policy? A policy that defines the types of gifts and assets Chrysalis will accept."

"I can live with that," Tom said, "as long as I have input into the final policy, then finance can get behind it."

> Craft a gift acceptance policy.

Chrysalis then took the next step on the **worthiness continuum**. Together, Tom and Jim crafted a gift acceptance policy to build a bridge between the efforts of Chrysalis's finance department and the development department. The policy outlined the types of assets they would accept as gifts, and it also clearly outlined how to deal with exceptions or unique circumstances. Jim and Tom agreed to work together as gifts came in, assuring that both teams understood the gift, the donor's objectives, and how the gift would ultimately benefit Chrysalis.

CELEBRATION

Jim studied himself in the mirror as he straightened his shirt and put on his tie. *Quite a few wrinkles*, he observed wryly. His thinning hair was now almost completely gray. *What a difference 20 years makes,* he thought. Funny, he still pictured himself as a much younger fundraising professional with fire in his belly and a runner's body!

Where had the time gone? Missy and Abigail are all grown up and married! he thought. *In fact, how cool that both will be at the special dinner tonight.*

He remembered those first five years as being pretty rough as he, Tom, and Koen worked flat out to get the train back on the track. *Yet,* he remembered, *those early efforts really paid off!* Koen's insistence on **organizational worthiness** paid growing dividends as donors developed a deepening trust in the organization and its leadership. Even more strategically, missionaries on the field experienced a growing confidence in the organization's management team. Jim used the gift planning tools and strategies he'd learned to help donors create increasingly complex gifting arrangements.

Those gift arrangements brought about the next step on **the worthiness continuum.**

While his fingers deftly knotted a conservative blue tie, his mind was far away as he thought back to an early discussion with Tom and where it had led them on this day of celebration.

A GOOD FIDUCIARY (20 YEARS AGO)

"This can't be happening," Jim groaned.

He marched into Tom's office and dropped into a chair.

Tom glanced at Jim over the top of his glasses. "The payments aren't right, and the donor's not happy with the portfolio! This really can't continue, Tom, I mean, I can't raise funds, engage donors, and deal with this banking team. They don't understand what we are trying to do here. They keep putting us in their institutional box and trying to make every trust we have look the same. In fact, I'm not sure they even care what the trust document says! This isn't what I'd call being a 'good fiduciary,'" Jim fumed.

Tom removed his glasses and began polishing them carefully. "Well," he said, "what do you suggest? We're getting a good deal on fees from the bank; they handle all our other banking business, and because of that larger relationship, they support us when it comes to investment consulting and planned gift administration."

"I know, I know," Jim grunted. "It's the same old story. But we're struggling to satisfy our donors. When I consider the situation holistically, I'm not sure that we're living up to our corporate values *or* our responsibility as a fiduciary and a steward!" he exclaimed.

Jim took a breath to calm himself, then started thinking out loud. "Maybe we need to look for another solution. I mean, we've worked so hard to get to this point, and I realize the bank plays an important role in providing traditional banking services to Chrysalis, but maybe they just aren't the best fit when it comes to assisting us with these noncash gifts."

Tom understood Jim's frustration. Over the last few years, Jim and his team had worked hard to build relationships with existing donors and to continue to add new Chrysalis donors. In the process, Jim had uncovered several more significant gifting opportunities and had convinced Tom and Koen to allow him to set up a gift annuity pool. Chrysalis also became the trustee of several charitable remainder trusts that Jim designed.

As Chrysalis's financial situation improved, Tom continued building a solid relationship with the bank. Naturally, as these more complex gift arrangements materialized, he simply leveraged the bank's other services to assist him in handling these new gifting vehicles. Now Jim was pushing back on this arrangement. In his own mind, Tom could acknowledge that their bank's solution did not benefit or engage donors, but it was simple, straightforward, and did not require an additional vendor.

"Jim, I see your point, but surely it can't be that bad. I mean, the bank manages hundreds if not thousands of trusts. Surely, their solution isn't a total disaster."

"Well," Jim said, "it seems pretty bad to me, and our donors aren't happy. The solutions the bank offers are not customized and often fail to fully meet the donors' expectations. Further, I can't get one of the bank's team members to help explain the investment solutions they create to our donors. It's hard to be excited about adding a new gift if we can't please our donors."

"That's true," Tom spoke thoughtfully as he replaced his glasses and looked across the desk at Jim.

"Tom, all I can say is that if we're ever going to hit that 50-million-dollar target Koen's set for the endowment, we are going to need a better solution!"

NEXT STEPS

Tom had put policies and procedures in place to help ensure that the funds gifted to Chrysalis were protected and well stewarded. Together, finance and development were doing a great job managing donor relationships and stewarding incoming gifts. However, the growing level of complex gifts and Jim's frustration with the bank led Koen to a growing realization that additional support and oversight were needed as the funds entrusted to the organization grew.

When Koen and Tom put together the finance and audit committee as a permanent subcommittee of the board, Koen believed the committee would be able to provide all the support that management needed. However, he could now see that meeting his long-term objective of a 50-million-dollar endowment required more oversight than the committee had the capacity to provide.

Like many nonprofit boards, Chrysalis's board comprised a broad mix of individuals, including entrepreneurs, CPAs, bankers, investment managers, pastors, and lawyers. When he and Tom put together the finance and audit committee, they had identified several key folks on the board to make up the committee.

They asked Tyler Jackson to chair the finance and audit committee. As a CPA and a long-time board member at Chrysalis, he believed in the vision and had worked hard to identify men and women from the board who could form that initial committee. It was Tyler who had worked out the details with the board regarding terms of service, voting, and reporting.

So, as Koen thought about the future and the complexity growth would bring, he decided he needed to set up a meeting with Tyler.

INVESTMENT COMMITTEE

Tyler took a sip of his black coffee. With his keen dark eyes, narrow face, and sharp features, Tyler resembled a hawk. In fact, Koen often felt he would hate to be on the wrong side of negotiations against Tyler! It seemed as though he could see right through you, to your soul.

"So," Tyler said, "Chrysalis is beginning to build up some funds?"

"Yes," Koen replied, "Jim's doing a great job. And you know, he's not only reaching out to our existing donors, but he's also started expanding our donor base. You remember that presentation he made to the board about estate planning?"

"Oh, yeah," Tyler sighed. "I guess I really need to learn more about that. I did hear the initial presentation, and it sounded great! But I failed to follow up with him."

"Don't worry about it, Tyler. Jim's just getting started, and I know he'll follow up with both you and the board as he gets this program rolling. Anyway, as Jim and I've been meeting with more donors, we've also been sharing our long-term vision to build an endowment.

"A number of current donors were intrigued with the idea, and that led Chrysalis into some complex gift arrangements. As part of Jim's development program, we've actually agreed to serve as trustee for several new charitable trusts, and the organization has begun to offer gift annuities to our constituents as well."

"Wow, that sounds great!" Tyler was clearly excited. "I noticed a few of those new gift arrangements when we reviewed the financial statements with the audit team. I've also noticed the general fund has continued to grow.

And, with the new missionaries Chrysalis has added, our missional reserve assets have increased as well. You and the team are doing a great job, Koen," Tyler said warmly.

"Thanks, Tyler, that's really part of why I'm here," Koen replied. "You see, as these assets continue to grow, we'll need more support and oversight to help steward the funds entrusted to us. Up to this point, I think we've done a great job building donor trust, offering transparency, and providing clear reporting on Chrysalis's work, but with the growth of our reserves and these new gift arrangements, I'm concerned we need more oversight, and soon."

Tyler leaned back in his chair, considering the problem. "Well, it's a good challenge to have, Koen, better than when we were swimming in red ink and up to our eyeballs in debt. That's for sure!"

Koen chuckled. "Yes, I'm glad those days are behind us, and Lord willing, we'll keep moving forward. But I do need your help, Tyler. How can we provide support to Chrysalis's management team in the oversight of these funds and also protect the interests of our donors?"

"What we need," Tyler announced, "is an investment committee. "

"An investment committee?" Koen seemed a bit skeptical.

"Yes," Tyler said definitively, "an investment committee. Another permanent subcommittee of the board that can specifically oversee the stewardship of Chrysalis's funds and work with management to ensure that the funds are invested in line with the objectives outlined in the gift arrangement or as outlined in Chrysalis's internal policies and procedures."

Tyler had an idea. "And you know, Koen, I think I have just the guy we're looking for. I think Doug McIntyre would be the perfect man for the job."

Koen thought about that for a moment. Doug McIntyre: solid, compact, knowledgeable. Doug was in his 70s now, but his career in the oil industry had taken him around the world and around the boardroom. Doug knew quite a bit about a lot of things and, maybe most importantly, he'd been involved with the investing world since he'd retired in his mid-60s. Doug had been a top-notch volunteer with Chrysalis for years: volunteering, giving financially, and serving on the board off and on over the years. He was currently back on and serving another term.

"You're right, Tyler. I think this could be a great role for Doug. I'll speak to him about it."

THE COMMITTEE CHAIR

Doug had recently moved from Texas to Georgia. So, on his next trip to Atlanta to meet with some donors, Koen set up a meeting with Doug. It was a cold day in early December when they met at Houston's restaurant in Buckhead. As always, Doug wore a tweed sport coat, newly pressed slacks, and a pair of Allen Edmonds dress shoes. Koen always noticed the shoes! Understated elegance, that was Doug to a T.

Koen arrived early for the appointment to find Doug already at the restaurant. *It seemed Doug was always one step ahead*, Koen thought amusedly. Doug gave him a firm handshake and led him to a table in the corner.

"What's on your mind, Koen?" Doug asked.

Koen didn't skip a beat and launched into the idea with little small talk. Over a nice lunch, he took the next hour to bring Doug up to speed on the fundraising efforts at Chrysalis.

"So, you see," Koen finished, "Tyler and I thought an investment committee might be the answer. What do you think?"

Doug was quiet for a few moments, thinking. "Well," he said slowly, "I think that could be a good strategic move for Chrysalis. You know, we want to do these things with excellence, Koen, we really do, and an investment committee could provide support for you, Tom, and Jim as these funds continue to grow. I think it's a good idea!"

"Great," Koen smiled, "because I was wondering if you would be willing to chair that committee and get it off the ground?"

Doug looked him straight in the eye. "I could do that!" he said enthusiastically. "In fact, I would welcome the opportunity to take on this project. It sounds like a great way for me to help Chrysalis, and I believe this is the best way for us to steward these assets."

Koen felt a tremendous sense of relief. Having Doug on board took a huge weight off his shoulders! He knew he could trust Doug to get into the details with Tom and Jim, and he knew that Doug would work to protect Chrysalis's donors while also keeping the board informed on the investment performance.

THE RIGHT INVESTMENT PARTNER

"Doug, now that you're on board and will be chairing the investment committee, I need to let you know that Tom and Jim have been discussing our current investment provider.

"I know that Jim's not happy with the current vendor we are utilizing in this area," Koen said. "Would you mind reaching out to Tom about the situation? He's been hesitant to change because he's comfortable with the bank. While he knows that Jim feels boxed in by the bank's structure, he also hates to complicate matters by adding another vendor."

"Sure, I'll reach out to him," Doug said. "CFOs are always comfortable with the bank," he smiled. "They usually build that relationship, and they work with the bank on all sorts of day-to-day issues from payroll to overseas wires. And, of course, the bank is only too happy to lower its fees in one area to grow the relationship in another area that generates more revenue for the bank. Maybe they *are* the right vendor, but maybe there are *other* alternatives that will offer more support and a better fit for what we want to accomplish at Chrysalis."

Not long after that meeting, Doug reached out to Tom, who knew Doug well from his various stints on the board. So, when the phone rang and Kristin buzzed to let him know that Doug was on the line, Tom was quick to take the call. "Good morning, Doug. What can I do for you this morning?"

"Morning, Tom," Doug said, "I had a meeting with Koen a week or so ago, and he's asked me to organize an investment committee for the board at Chrysalis."

"Great to hear from you, Doug. Yes, Koen and I had discussed how, as the ministry grows, we need to grow our approach. I like our current systems and practices, but I also understand how complicated stewarding large gifts is. I really liked the idea of having an investment committee, and I'm encouraged that your leadership will help set its course. I definitely want to help in any way I can, but I also want you to know that change won't be easy. We have a really great partnership with the bank."

Doug thought he heard a bit of concern in Tom's voice and wondered if he might be concerned that Doug intended to start throwing his weight around and disrupt Tom's system.

"Tom, I know you, Jim, and Koen have made tremendous strides at Chrysalis! The way the three of you've managed to turn this situation around is nothing short of miraculous. I know the board is thrilled, and I'm thrilled with the results you've been able to generate. You've done a great job building infrastructure to support the organization's financial growth, and I appreciate the way you have honed in on cost control. We can't control everything, but we can certainly work hard to be sure that we are careful with our spending."

Doug's words went a long way toward alleviating Tom's concern. *Maybe Koen's solution wasn't so bad after all.*

"Well, the investment side is new for me," Tom admitted. "I think we have a decent plan in place to handle the funds entrusted to us, but I have to admit that Jim's not thrilled with our current vendor."

"Why do you think that is?" Doug asked.

"Jim keeps saying he feels 'institutionalized.' He feels like the bank simply puts all of our investment portfolios in the same box. Jim is pursuing more donors, and he's pursuing them more holistically, which is leading to different types of gifts. Asset-based gifts, trusts, gift annuities, it's all a bit beyond me.

"And while the bank has a trust department providing both the investment management and administration for these vehicles, Jim doesn't feel they are being managed well. It seems as though the bank really isn't providing much support. But, you know, the bank does quite a bit for us; it's an important relationship.

"They help provide us with an interest-bearing sweep, wire funds to our teams overseas, support our payroll process, and provide a line of credit. They are important!" Tom spoke just a bit defensively.

"No doubt, they are important," Doug soothed. "But maybe they are not the best alternative for everything."

"Well, that could be," Tom said, "I just hate to be tasked with managing another vendor."

"I can certainly understand that!" Doug laughed.

"I remember when I was working at Occidental Petroleum, the last thing I wanted to do was bring on yet another vendor. But you know, Tom, if we can find the *right* vendor in this space, I believe that vendor will seem more like a partner than a vendor."

"Maybe so," Tom still sounded somewhat dubious. "Where do we go from here?" he asked.

"I'm just getting my arms around all this as well." Doug's voice was reassuring and warm, "I think the next step is to have a conversation with Jim so we can get his input. How about I get hold of Jim? I'll reach out to Kristin. I'm sure she can help us get some time on your calendar there at headquarters," Doug said.

"Okay, that sounds good," Tom said. As he laid down his phone, Tom felt better and could feel himself smiling. *Maybe Doug will actually help us do this better!*

CONSULTANT REVIEW

Doug was as good as his word. A couple of weeks later, he, Tom, and Jim met up at Chrysalis's headquarters in Greenville.

Jim met Doug at the door and gave him a quick tour of the building. "You know we've fully paid off the debt on the building!" Jim said enthusiastically.

"That's fantastic," Doug said. "You, Koen, and Tom have done a great job getting Chrysalis back on track and moving in the right direction."

"Well, you know I attribute a lot of it to Koen's vision for the organization, coupled with his obsession with **worthiness!"** Jim beamed.

"Oh, yeah," Doug grinned. "He's definitely been riding that horse. I think he's brought it up at every board meeting I've ever been in. But it looks as though it must be working!"

"Yeah, I really think it is," Jim said. "I'm truly beginning to see the way that our organizational worthiness impacts the ability to raise funds and earn donors' trust.

Koen began his tenure here at Chrysalis by defining what he meant by worthiness.

"His first step was to be sure we were all very clear about Chrysalis's vision, mission, and values. Our vision: *we exist to offer the hope of Jesus Christ to those displaced by armed conflict around the world!* And our mission: *to provide food, shelter, and the message of Christ's love to human beings displaced by armed conflict around the globe.* He taught us that an organization's vision is often the first thing that attracts a potential donor.

"Once we got that down, he and Tom beefed up Chrysalis's financial infrastructure. We joined ECFA and initiated an annual audit. Tom and the finance team also built an internal policy governance structure around our donation management.

"We added the finance and audit committee and, more recently, Tom and I nailed down a gift acceptance policy around the gifts we're willing to accept from our donors, as well as exceptions to that policy."

Doug looked impressed. "It seems to me that Koen's initiation of this new investment committee is the logical next step in the, what does he call it, the **worthiness process?**"

"The **worthiness continuum**," it was Jim's turn to grin. "Hard to forget that around here! We hear about it all the time." Jim mimicked Koen's exuberant expressions, "We've got to keep Chrysalis moving along **the worthiness continuum**!

"And you know," Jim said, "it is clearly working. I'm excited about this investment committee, and I'm grateful you are willing to chair it, Doug. We need your help!

"I'm realizing more and more added components to worthiness that donors care about. I believe these other elements go beyond organizational worthiness and relate to the personal worthiness of the fundraiser. People give to people, Doug. But before I can really get comfortable moving forward with this more holistic approach to donor engagement I've been exploring, we've got to get the right partners in place to help us steward the assets entrusted to us."

"That's why I'm here," Doug smiled.

When they came to the conference room door, Doug shook Tom's hand and, while taking a seat, he thought seriously about what Jim had said.

Doug, Tom, and Jim met for a couple of hours. They reviewed the current investable reserves managed by the bank, along with the trusts and gift annuity program. They had a lot to review and discuss.

Jim expressed his concerns about being 'institutionalized,' and Tom had the chance to share his worries about vendor management and Chrysalis's overall relationship with the bank. Doug listened to Tom sympathetically and highlighted his and Jim's desire for a true partner in this area.

Jim explained how an investment team could provide the skilled investment consulting and administrative support Chrysalis needed to bring on more gift arrangements as they pursued greater donor engagement. Of course, cost was factored into the equation, and they also discussed the importance of this partner understanding the estate-planning process, including charitable gift types. A good partner could even assist Jim in the structure and completion of these types of gifts.

While cash giving to Chrysalis continued to increase, they clearly needed to build out their asset-based giving and planned giving to meet their long-term endowment goal. Consequently, their preferred partner needed to demonstrate expertise in each of these areas. Finally, they agreed that it would be extremely helpful if their financial partner shared their value system.

As they discussed this element in the decision-making process, they realized it took on greater significance than it had initially appeared. While it was true that Chrysalis's donors were inclined to generosity, the key component of their giving had its foundations in their Christian faith.

All three men realized the supremacy of this element: that their prospective partner must share their value system. Most often, a financial consultant and investment partner acted as a silent partner. However, they started considering how many scenarios could arise where that partner would come in contact with the Chrysalis donor base. At those crucial times, a shared value system would undoubtedly lead to greater connection and trust on the part of the donor.

Jim became quite emphatic on that point. "We are acting as a steward to stewards," he said. "I need a partner who understands that stewardship responsibility, is skilled at investment management, and is just as skilled at helping donors implement their charitable plans.

"I see too many investment teams who are more concerned with their assets under management than with money flowing to the Kingdom. We need a partner who wants to see Kingdom purposes funded every bit as much as we do!"

By the end of the meeting, the key elements of investment customization, flexibility, and shared values had convinced Tom that they must seek a new investment partner.

The bank would, of course, remain an important part of Chrysalis's financial infrastructure. They hammered out the list of questions they would pose to prospective firms in their request for proposal (RFP). Then they agreed that Doug would lead the search process on behalf of Chrysalis.

All three of them had started a list of prospective firms to whom they could send the RFP. But Tom and Jim also agreed to check out one particular candidate who had reached out to Chrysalis, offering services in this area. They both remembered the firm, FAC, because it offered both investment consulting and gift administration. From what they remembered, the firm's management shared its value system.

REQUEST FOR PROPOSAL

Doug quickly got the RFP process going, and over the next few weeks, responses started coming in. As he, Tom, and Jim reviewed the proposals from several firms, they included their bank in the RFP process as well. It quickly became apparent to all of them, *even Tom*, that the bank did not fit the ideal candidate they had in mind, but several other firms looked promising.

One large, independent consulting firm based out of Atlanta seemed attractive, but with less than ten million in assets, Chrysalis would barely meet their minimum, not to mention that they couldn't handle the administrative component of the trusts and gift annuity program.

Another candidate, affiliated with a major wirehouse, seemed like a reasonable option. They partnered with an outside "administration only" team to collaborate on a fairly attractive proposal.

There was another secular team that seemed to have all the answers, offering both asset management consulting and administration done in-house. In addition, they certainly seemed to understand the planned giving space. The main drawbacks were the price, which seemed expensive, and again, Chrysalis barely met its minimum asset requirement. Chrysalis did intend to grow, however, and after a good deal of conversation, Jim, Tom, and Doug decided to invite the firm, SC Investment Management, to the finals.

And then there was FAC.

Tom and Jim had met with FAC before and were impressed at the time, but at that meeting, Tom still felt comfortable at the bank, and Jim had been content with that decision. This time, however, they had a more earnest intention of finding a new partner and were anxious to see how Doug responded to FAC's RFP material.

Doug was impressed. As a reasonably-sized boutique firm out of Atlanta, FAC offered both investment consulting and charitable gift administration in-house. They also indicated their ability to work with charities in accepting more complex gifts. Their responses to the RFP clearly indicated that they shared Chrysalis's value system, and while they were somewhat smaller than the other candidates, they showed convincing proof of retaining experienced consultants and had experience with other well-known, faith-based clients.

"I think FAC should be our other finalist," Doug said.

"Great." Jim felt a sense of relief. He'd wanted FAC to make the finals, but didn't want to push too hard. Since Doug took the lead on the investment committee, Jim wanted this relationship to get off on the right foot. He was pleased, nonetheless, that Doug saw value in this firm.

"Tom, what do you think?" Doug asked.

"Oh, I'm fine, including them, Doug. I think they are a good candidate, but I'm concerned that they will complicate our processes unnecessarily. I'm interested to see them present to the board. As a boutique, they might be able to offer us specialized services, but I'm concerned they might not be fully equipped with enough resources to meet our specific needs. If they can prove they can meet our needs, I can get on board." Tom said.

Chrysalis had a board meeting coming up in the next month. They planned to have the finalists make a presentation to the entire board at the meeting.

THE CONSULTANT

Liam, the CEO of FAC, was nervous! His company's logo on the screen held center stage in front of a packed boardroom of well-dressed men and women, buzzing with conversations and waiting to hear more. It wasn't as though he hadn't presented to a board before, but he understood the significance of this opportunity.

Aware of the obvious growth taking place with Chrysalis, he remembered when Warren, his Chief Operating Officer, and Kathy, his Director of Marketing, had met with Chrysalis only a few years ago. At that time, Chrysalis was still happy with the bank and perhaps had the impression that FAC was too small.

He and Kathy had built the beginnings of a relationship with Jim, and Liam felt certain that small beginnings had influenced Chrysalis to re-engage as they looked for a new partner. Now that the chips were down, FAC needed to convince the Chrysalis board that they were the right team to partner with to grow with them in the future.

As Liam walked to the front of the room, not a hint of his nerves could be seen. The board only saw a tall, lean, blue-eyed man with short blond hair and a well-tailored suit. His features were a bit sharp, and he gave off an air of intensity, perhaps just a bit too intense, some thought. He walked quickly to the front of the room and introduced himself to the board. He took a moment to introduce Warren and Kathy to the group and then indicated that in the interest of time, he would be spearheading FAC's presentation to the board.

Liam noted FAC was an independent financial consulting firm registered with the SEC. He outlined FAC's service model. The firm focused its efforts in three distinct areas: investment consulting, planned-gift administration, and planned-gift consulting.

Over the next 30 minutes, Liam explained to the board that FAC focused its sales efforts on faith-based organizations like Chrysalis.

FAC, he said, believed strongly that each pool of assets entrusted to the organization should have its own investment policy framework. A master policy governing all Chrysalis funds was helpful, he explained, but each pool needed its own unique investment policy outlining the pertinent goals, objectives, and constraints. Each pool should follow a strategic asset allocation to meet specific goals and objectives.

Liam explained that the first step was for the board at Chrysalis to agree on an investment philosophy that would drive the overall investment program for Chrysalis. That philosophy would help ensure the development of the board's unique worldview of investments. This philosophy would define significant investment management-related beliefs. For example, would Chrysalis prioritize active or passive investments? Would tactical asset allocation be an acceptable technique? What level of risk would be appropriate? What did Chrysalis's board believe about values-based investing?

These issues, Liam advised, should be clearly articulated, allowing the board's broader values to influence each individual investment policy. "FAC will work with your board to develop an investment philosophy if you haven't already created one. Then, we'll guide you through the process of developing individual investment policy statements—road maps, if you will—to guide the implementation of each pool's investment strategy." This process, he explained, would help provide clarity and transparency for donors while also providing clear guidelines and benchmarks for the board's oversight.

Liam went on to say that this process allowed investment pools, like charitable trusts or gift annuity pools with their corresponding liabilities, to be invested differently from one another. "FAC believes this approach is critical. All funds entrusted to Chrysalis are associated with a corresponding cash flow liability. In the case of a charitable trust, for example, a donor receives income from the trust, but ultimately, at maturity, the assets go to charity. As trustee, Chrysalis must take both of these factors into account. As fiduciary for these assets, Chrysalis is ultimately responsible to those beneficiaries regarding the outcome of the investment.

"However," Liam reassured the board, "we act as a co-fiduciary with our clients! As co-fiduciary, we sit on the same side of the table as you, and our interests are aligned with yours. A significant part of our mission is to preserve, grow, and distribute the assets entrusted to nonprofits like Chrysalis for the purpose of enhancing their organizational stewardship." Clearly, Liam was passionate about this topic. "Like other consultants," he said, "we have significant skill in the areas of portfolio design, manager selection, and reporting. This focus on liability-driven investment management makes us distinctive!

"Additionally, as fiduciary and trustee, Chrysalis is responsible for ensuring that donors receive distributions from their charitable trust, gift annuity, pooled income fund (PIF), or other vehicle. In the case of an endowment, donors want to know their funds are being invested properly with the correct amount distributed each year to fund the causes specified in the endowment agreement. FAC's investment team and administrative team work closely together to help ensure distributions go out on time and the portfolio is continually rebalanced. Ensuring that tax returns and 1099s are delivered on time is another important part of our role. We'll work closely with Jim and his team, supporting donors. Setting proper expectations and delivering on those expectations will help Chrysalis build a happy and satisfied donor base.

"Remember," Liam said, "this business is all about trust! Chrysalis must be able to trust its consultant, and donors must be able to trust Chrysalis!

"FAC is here to do just that. We want to help Chrysalis expand its donor engagement so you can fund your mission and vision. That's how we see our job: helping you achieve excellence in financial stewardship.

"This will ultimately result in more dollars funding Kingdom impact. This is how we make your vision a reality, as a team. While FAC often functions as a silent back office, we can also come alongside Jim and the development department to assist in closing various asset-based and planned gift arrangements. With over 30 years of experience, our team is here to support you."

MAKING THE CHOICE

Following the finalists' presentations, the board discussed the candidates. Jim and Tom weren't voting members, but the board respected their opinions.

Tom was a bit uncertain. The larger firm was polished and certainly looked good on paper. It was also clear that Chrysalis would just be a number to them. Furthermore, that firm's investment solutions did not appear to be any more sophisticated than FAC's. FAC had the advantage here, as they clearly understood Chrysalis's value system.

Jim spoke with confidence, "FAC is the best fit for us. I can work with them. They'll make excellent partners. They understand what we're trying to do and where we're trying to go. I met Liam's teammate, Warren, and he clearly understands all the nuances related to our desire to be worthy of donors' trust, and their team can help us with specifics like trust management, gift administration, and gift annuity programs, along with other types of gift arrangements like donor advised funds. I think FAC is the way to go," he finished.

Doug waited for other board members to share their thoughts, and then he asked Koen to share his thoughts.

Koen smiled, "I defer to your leadership on this, Doug, but I have to say, I believe the FAC team will naturally understand how we are working to make Chrysalis worthy in the eyes of our donors. As we keep moving along the worthiness continuum, FAC can help us take the steps necessary to reassure our donors that we are competent fiduciaries capable of stewarding the funds they entrust to us."

"Okay," Doug weighed in, "while it seems like a few folks were comfortable with SC Investments, the majority of us seem to be leaning toward FAC. I also like FAC," he said. "I can work with them to develop philosophy, policy, and a reporting framework that can be overseen by our new investment committee."

The chairman of the board took the matter to a vote, and it was determined that FAC would become the new Chrysalis investment consultant and administrative solution for planned gifts.

The board moved on to other matters, and Jim left the meeting. He felt relieved and excited. He hadn't realized how much was riding on the board's decision. The situation with the bank had been weighing on his mind, but he hadn't realized how heavily. Now that Chrysalis had decided on a new partner, and one Jim felt could help him get to the next level, he could feel the excitement rising inside him. Now he had the confidence to take the next step along the worthiness continuum and really begin building the fundraising program at Chrysalis. He could fully employ all that he was learning about major donor development, current giving, and planned gift design.

He felt as though the sky was the limit!

CELEBRATION

Jim put on his sports coat and stood waiting for Ann.

"You look wonderful," he told her. When he looked at her, it was hard to believe that he was already in his late 60s. "Ann," he said, "you just keep looking younger all the time! Everyone is going to think I robbed the cradle!"

"Well, you are getting pretty old," Ann teased. "I mean, you can hardly make it down the stairs these days!" She pushed him out the door. "Come on, old man, let's get this day started right."

Together they hurried down to breakfast. This tenth anniversary President's Weekend was special. The team decided to go all out. Even stodgy old Tom had agreed that they could spend some money to celebrate.

Breakfast at the Ritz is always a sumptuous affair, and this breakfast was no exception. Strawberries, blueberries, pineapple, and small pieces of kiwi fruit artfully arranged on silver platters rested on a long table. Nearby, an omelet station and a Belgian waffle station bookended Jim's favorite: cheese blintzes with raspberry compote.

Jim and Ann ran into Koen while they were in line for an omelet. The past 25 years had been kind to Koen, Jim thought. Although he had recently lost his wife to cancer, he looked healthy, happy, and energetic. Despite his age, his hair was still dark, and it didn't seem to Jim like he had put on a single pound. His dark, intense eyes twinkled with excitement as he related to Jim that he had just spoken with Mary Pat Kingston, one of their first major donors. Koen had first met Mary Pat when he joined Chrysalis 25 years ago, and now he shared how excited she was to be part of this event.

"She just can't wait to hear what we're up to!" Koen said. "It is really amazing how invested she is in our mission."

"Yeah," Jim said, "she's been such a staunch supporter all these years. I'm glad she felt well enough to come."

"I've got to run," Koen said. "I'll catch up with you later today!"

Jim and Ann headed off to a table populated with other Chrysalis donors. While Ann talked with donors, many of whom were now like old friends, Jim looked around the room. They had invited over 100 couples to the event this year, their largest yet, and he was thrilled with the turnout. He was also a bit nervous. What was Koen going to announce?

As he recognized face after face, he found his mind drifting back again to that transitional period when Chrysalis first began working with FAC and Doug began building the investment committee.

INVESTMENT PHILOSOPHY (20 YEARS AGO)

After the board meeting, Doug and Tom notified FAC that they had been selected as Chrysalis's new investment consultant. The FAC team noted that, as they worked through the transition of the assets with Tom's finance team, they also needed to work with the Chrysalis team to hammer out investment philosophy and policy. Doug and Tom agreed this was the purview of the newly formed investment committee. Doug would coordinate with FAC to get the new documents created. Rather than go back and forth via phone and email, Doug preferred to visit FAC's office in Atlanta to solidify the details. The FAC team was thrilled. Having Doug on site would allow them to begin building a relationship with him, and it would allow them to expeditiously build Chrysalis's philosophy and investment policies on a comprehensive basis.

A couple of weeks later, Doug visited the FAC office. The FAC team rolled out the red carpet for him. The entire team was on hand to greet him, and he sat down in a well-appointed conference room with Liam and Warren to begin work on the Chrysalis investment philosophy.

"So," Doug said, "tell me more about investment philosophy. I'm not sure I've ever heard it referred to that way."

Liam walked over to the whiteboard and began to write as he spoke, "What are our core beliefs about investing, and how will our beliefs affect the funds that have been entrusted to us?

"This is the core question we need to answer, Doug," Liam said. "In spiritual terms, we might think of this as Chrysalis's 'World View' of investing. We want to get this nailed down because, over time, the people who comprise the investment committee and management at Chrysalis will change. Each new member or employee will have his or her own view of how to invest money, and we don't want our strategy in flux. Over the next few hours, we want to define our core beliefs about investing the money entrusted to Chrysalis. Those beliefs will inform policy and will ultimately drive how our assets are invested."

Liam headed back to the board and wrote, "Asset allocation."

"So," he said, "at FAC, we believe in long-term structural allocation modeling. We believe that how we allocate assets among large asset classes like stocks, bonds, alternative assets, and cash drives most of a portfolio's return. It also drives the bulk of the variance in that portfolio's return. An asset class's return is related to its volatility, and a more volatile asset class should produce higher returns. If it doesn't, we should avoid that asset class. The real challenge is that it is difficult to time when to be in one asset class instead of another."

"Good," Doug spoke up. "I was worried we were going to have to argue about tactical asset allocation and market timing. I certainly don't believe in trying to time the market or putting all our money in a single asset class, no matter how well we think it's going to do."

"That makes three of us!" Warren laughed.

"I'm glad we are all on the same page," said Liam. "So, we're agreed. The first point in Chrysalis's investment philosophy will indicate the belief in strategic asset allocation."

"You know," Doug said, "I do believe that there are times we might want to tilt toward or away from a given asset class. For example, if interest rates are low, bonds or cash might not be as attractive. How do we address that?"

"Great question," Liam answered. "We believe that 'tactical tilts' can be applied within the broader strategic asset allocation model without violating the organization's philosophical position. We address these issues more specifically by applying ranges in the investment policy documents."

"Okay, sounds good," Doug responded. "Let's keep moving."

"The next key philosophical point relates to active versus passive investment management," Warren noted.

Liam wrote, "Active vs Passive," on the whiteboard.

"By 'active' you mean trying to use stock or bond managers to outperform the market?" Doug confirmed.

"Exactly," Warren answered. "Here at FAC, we can implement a portfolio's allocation actively, passively, or with a combination approach we refer to as core satellite."

"Well, I have to admit my view on this one is somewhat mixed," Doug hesitated. "I believe that sometimes managers can add value, but it seems like some markets may be too efficient for a manager to really win."

"We understand that position," Warren said. "It really comes from the efficient market hypothesis."

"What is that?" Doug asked.

Liam rolled his eyes. "Really, Warren, you just had to go there," he groaned.

"Well, sometimes a little theory goes a long way," Warren said.

"Anyway," Liam went on, "what Warren is trying to say is that some markets price assets efficiently, and in those markets it may make sense to passively replicate the market rather than try to beat it."

"I see," Doug said. "So, for example, in a market like the United States S&P 500, big stocks like Apple, Coke, and Tesla are difficult to outperform, right?"

"Exactly," Warren answered. "In those markets, we can implement a passive approach, but in other smaller capitalization markets or emerging markets, we may choose a more active approach. The other benefit, of course, is that passive management is cheaper."

"That makes sense to me," Doug said. "From my knowledge of the board at Chrysalis, I think we would lean toward your core satellite approach. In certain markets, where pricing is already very efficient, active management doesn't make sense. We would rather go with a cheaper passive option."

"Let's talk about diversification for a moment," Liam said.

"Oh, I don't think we need to spend much time on that one," Doug broke in. "Of course, we have to be diversified. We are fiduciaries. We might win big by putting all our eggs in one basket, but we would look pretty foolish if something happened to that basket!"

It was Warren's turn to laugh. "That's right, Doug. In the fiduciary world, we have a guideline for that, too. It's called the Uniform Prudent Management of Institutional Funds Act, or UPMIFA for short. It says what you just said. Institutional fiduciaries need to utilize diversification to demonstrate prudency. Incidentally, the act also states that a fiduciary must take costs into account and endowment distributions should be set at a sustainable level.

"We outline that in the investment policy documents as well," Warren finished.

"Great," Doug said. "Guys, I feel like we are making real progress here! What's next?"

"Well," Liam said, "the final philosophical element is related to 'values-based investing.'"

"Is that related to ESG?" Doug asked.

"Yes, it is," Warren answered, "but there is a lot of confusion around ESG and values-based investing. That's why we believe Chrysalis needs to clarify its philosophical position on these issues."

"Okay," Doug said, "you'll have to help me understand this and how it affects our portfolios. While I've heard of ESG, I'm not really sure what it means!"

Liam smiled, "ESG stands for Environmental, Social, and Governance."

"Well, those areas certainly seem important," Doug said.

"Yes, they are, but they can also confuse investors and affect stock or bond selection. For example, we might all agree that a company must care for the environment as it goes about its business, but the level of care and the impact of that concern may be reflected differently in different companies, industries, and sectors of the market."

"Oh, I see," Doug broke in. "When I was working in the oil industry, some investors avoided our stock simply because we were involved in carbon-based energy production!"

"Exactly," Liam exclaimed. "Different organizations and investors can express their values by carefully choosing which stocks to own. Most investment teams choose individual stocks and bonds in line with their values. They consider environmental issues, social issues, and corporate governance issues along with valuation, growth, and other traditional security selection metrics. However, when an organization asks a manager to go deeper in a particular area, we refer to this as values-based investing. An organization may, for example, ask a manager to avoid a company that produces tobacco-based products as its primary line of business because it believes that tobacco products are harmful to humans. They're willing to forgo the profit they could earn by investing in a company primarily involved in the production of those products.

Some organizations might eschew corporate casino holders because they believe gambling has a negative impact on society. Traditionally, the avoidance of these types of companies has been referred to as a negative screen.

"Another way an organization can reflect its values through its investments is impact-based investing. Rather than relying solely on negative screening, an organization may employ a manager to deploy positive value-based criteria in its selection methodology. For example, an organization like Chrysalis could look for a manager who is not only evaluating companies based on traditional financial metrics but also looking for companies that promote human flourishing or perhaps are providing unique employment opportunities in war-torn communities."

"This does sound like an important element for us to address from a philosophical perspective," Doug said. "It also sounds like it can be both challenging and nuanced!"

"Absolutely," Warren replied. "Values-driven investing is not always black and white. In some cases, it can be very difficult to implement. However, the good news is that awareness is increasing. Many investment teams offer screening solutions that align with Chrysalis's value system. What's most important is that the organization considers these issues and clearly articulates its position! This allows donors to understand the organization's point of view and helps build trust with constituents."

"I can see how that would be the case," Doug said. "A values-aligned approach certainly fits into the theme of worthiness that Koen is focused on. Chrysalis would want to take a best-efforts approach in this area," Doug indicated. "Wherever possible, we want to avoid direct investment in companies that derive a significant portion of their revenue from gambling, pornography, or tobacco. We would like to seek out investment selection methodologies that align with our value system from an impact perspective."

"Great," Warren agreed. "We can flesh this out more as we move into creating investment policies for Chrysalis's individual portfolios."

"This has been a great morning." Doug was energized by the process and excited to get these key philosophical concepts down on paper!

"Yep. We've gotten a lot done. Why don't we head to lunch? This afternoon, we can dive into policy formation," Liam suggested.

INVESTMENT POLICY

As they settled back into the conference room following lunch, Doug recapped the morning's work. "We have our key philosophical objectives:

"**Diversification** is essential for the protection of Chrysalis's assets.

"**Long-term strategic allocation** drives the majority of portfolio returns. While Chrysalis may tilt its investment portfolio to take advantage of market opportunities, it will not engage in aggressive tactical allocation or market timing.

"At Chrysalis, we believe both **active and passive management** solutions have their place in portfolio management and may be deployed when implementing Chrysalis's investment policies.

"Whenever possible, Chrysalis will seek to **reflect its values** through its investment program.

"**Cost control is essential,** and Chrysalis will work with its investment managers and consultants to ensure the cost of implementation remains reasonable and commensurate with services provided.

"How do we incorporate these 'big picture ideals' into our policy framework?"

"Great question," Warren answered. "Investment policies are written for each portfolio. They reference Chrysalis's philosophical beliefs and go one step further. We distill those beliefs into an implementable portfolio solution."

"You know," Doug reflected, "it kind of seems like overkill to have to write a policy for every portfolio. Is that really necessary?"

"I can understand why it might seem unnecessary. You might think having an overarching policy is enough, but this next piece is critical," Liam exclaimed. "Let me share a story with you to illustrate why investment policies are so important for organizations like Chrysalis:

"A donor set up a charitable trust and requested a very high payout. Each year, a charitable remainder unitrust resets its value, typically on January 1. This means that each year, a new distribution amount is set, based on the value of the trust.

In this case, the donor requested a 10 percent standard payout arrangement, which means each year the trust is required to distribute 10 percent back to the donor's family. That level of distribution is extremely high, and it created a liquidity constraint that made long-term growth objectives very difficult to achieve. The charitable trustee would have a difficult time balancing the required payout to the income beneficiary with preservation of the principal of the trust for future distribution to charity.

"The organization requested a discussion with the donor to help him understand it was very likely that, over time, the principal would decline as the annual payment to the income beneficiaries was made. The donor said, 'No problem. I understand. I plan to give my annual

distributions back to charity, and I am choosing this high payout arrangement so I can do more of my giving now rather than after I die. Of course, what's left in the trust will go to charity as well. This is really an entirely charitable vehicle.

My family does not need the income from this trust.'

"Shortly thereafter, the donor died while away on a business trip. His wife, the secondary income beneficiary, became the primary upon his death. This was during a time of significant economic and market decline. The trust, which had generally been keeping up with the required payments to the family and maintaining its overall principal value,

declined significantly due to the decline in equity markets.

"Initially, the trust was invested aggressively to keep up with the 10 percent payout. Of course, it fell significantly during the market's decline, approximately 35 percent when factoring in the trust's distribution. The trust declined from around a million dollars to $650,000 over the course of that one year. When the trust reset at the beginning of the next year, the payment to his wife dropped from approximately $100,000 to $65,000.

"The family was very concerned about this significant decline in the distribution and wondered if the charity was acting improperly as a fiduciary. The family contacted the charity to voice their concerns.

"Thankfully, the charity had an investment policy statement in place, and they had documented the original conversation with the donor in the policy's summary.

"As it turned out, the family misunderstood the type of gift their father created. They believed he had created a gift annuity, ensuring an annual payment of $100,000 regardless of any change in principal value. Once they understood the situation and were able to

review the policy, they accepted the charity's decisions. The portfolio was on course. It had simply gone through a difficult period. As the markets rebounded, the portfolio rebounded significantly.

"We could share similar stories about endowments, pooled income funds, and donor advised funds. Investment policy statements provide an essential framework to align the interests of all stakeholders in a particular portfolio," Liam finished.

"Wow, that's quite a story." Doug sat for a minute, reflecting. "An investment policy is part of our responsibility as an investment fiduciary. It will help demonstrate our organization's worthiness to our donors. I suppose each policy will look a bit different, but there must be some key elements that are in every policy, right?"

"Quite right," Warren noted in his precise manner.

Liam smiled. "Yes, Doug, some key components should be included in every investment policy."

Warren headed back to the whiteboard and wrote, "Summary – each policy should contain a summary of the overall purpose and juxtaposition of the funds."

Doug grinned. Only Warren would use a word like *juxtaposition,* he thought. "Okay, I get it," he said. "We need to summarize the situation!"

"Exactly," Warren beamed. He wrote, "Objectives," on the whiteboard. "Each policy should outline the objectives of that pool of assets," he lectured.

Below "Objectives," he wrote, "Constraints."

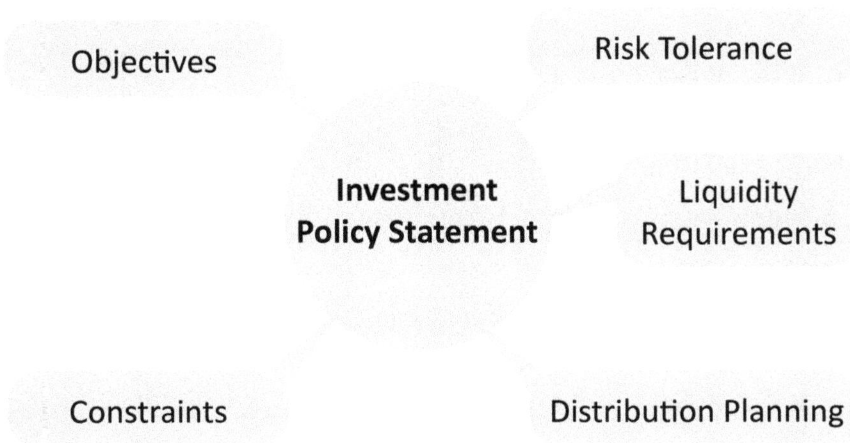

"Constraints are really important," Warren continued, "because they explain the limitations that may impact how we implement an investment plan for a specific portfolio. We generally want to account for the following key components: risk tolerance, liquidity requirements, distribution planning, and any legal and regulatory constraints or unique circumstances that may affect portfolio implementation," writing each on the board as he spoke. "This is where we make comments regarding social screening and faith-based investing.

"Finally, a summary of acceptable investment alternatives should be included." Warren was rarely happier than when he got the opportunity to lecture on his favorite topic. "Then," he began.

"Oh, really," Doug interrupted. "There's more?"

Warren stared at Doug for a moment. Then it dawned on him that Doug was giving him a hard time. "Well!" he huffed, shrugging and turning a bit red at the same time. "I guess it isn't the most riveting summary."

Doug and Liam both laughed.

"No, no," Doug chuckled. "You're doing great. Please forgive me, Warren. Keep going."

Somewhat mollified, Warren continued. "Well, there's really not too much more," he sighed. "The objectives and constraints section should lead to a target strategic asset allocation. That is, there should be a section of the investment policy statement outlining how much exposure to various asset classes like stocks, bonds, cash, commodities, and real estate are acceptable. A range around these values is important because it helps ensure that the portfolio does not unintentionally take on unnecessary risk while also guaranteeing the oversight team doesn't violate our philosophical belief about market timing."

"Great!" Doug said. He was feeling a bit sheepish for ribbing Warren. To make up for it, he tried to appear excited as he asked, "Is there anything else we need to include?"

"That's about it," Warren said. "The last element of the policy is a note regarding planned implementation. We highlight how the asset allocation will be implemented via active or passive investment alternatives like exchange-traded funds, mutual funds, separately managed investment accounts, and alternatives like private equity or hedge funds. That sort of thing," Warren concluded.

"Thanks for that very thorough explanation," Doug said. "This has been extremely helpful and informative." He looked at Liam, "How do we get these in place for each of Chrysalis's portfolios?"

"Well," Liam said, "now that you have helped us nail down your investment philosophy, our team will put together draft policies for the Chrysalis investment committee to review and approve. Often, for new charitable trusts, it is important to include the income beneficiary in the discussion as well. With donor advised funds, the situation is a bit different. In those situations, the donor picks from pre-defined investment portfolios that have already been approved by the investment committee. Or in the case of a larger gift, a unique policy and portfolio may be required."

REPORTING

"Okay, great. I think I've got it. Let's move forward with those policy drafts," Doug agreed. "This has been a very productive day, and I've learned a tremendous amount. I'm excited about getting these policies in place and preparing the committee to begin its oversight function. How do we monitor this?"

"Great point, Doug." Liam was impressed. "The next step is to create a reporting structure to keep key stakeholders informed and ensure all elements of the process are functioning as expected.

"There's an old adage," Liam quipped. "'What gets measured gets done!' We set up a reporting program that allows the investment committee to monitor the investment program and track investment objectives. This enables us to report back to other stakeholders, like donors and income beneficiaries, regarding their gift arrangements.

"A good reporting strategy relies on three key elements." It was Liam's turn to head to the whiteboard. He wrote, "Align, Focus, and Communicate.

"First, we need to build our reports to **align** with our audience," he said. "For example, a report for the investment committee will be more detailed and contain more specific information than a report to the general board."

"That makes sense," Doug said.

"We need to communicate the right information to stakeholders like donors or income beneficiaries. We don't want to overload them with detail or lead them to incorrect conclusions regarding their own responsibilities related to their gift."

"I think I see," said Doug. "A simple high-level report indicating how the organization has utilized a donor's gift to fulfill the vision and mission may be enough in the case of an outright gift. With a more sophisticated arrangement like a charitable trust or endowment gift, more reporting may be required."

"Exactly," Liam said. "We want to be sure the stakeholder receives the proper information. We want to build trust without overwhelming them in the process!"

"What do you mean by the second word, 'Focus'?" Doug asked.

"Reporting should **focus on results**," Liam answered. "As a steward of the funds entrusted to it, Chrysalis has a fiduciary responsibility to donors and constituents. Results might relate to ministry objectives or to specific financial results relevant to a donor's gift arrangement."

"Context is always important," Liam noted. "Remember, the donor is a steward as well. They feel responsible for the money they have entrusted to Chrysalis in the form of their gift. Context includes the state of the environment in which Chrysalis is operating. In the case of a financial report, context is referred to as 'benchmarking.' We want to provide the reader with the proper context in which to evaluate the results generated."

"Okay," Doug replied, "I think I see what you mean. For example, if a global pandemic hinders our ability to fully engage in certain regions of the world, we would want to highlight that 'context' when reporting back to our donors."

"That's correct. Or, if the stock market is down 20 percent for the year, we want to provide that information to a stakeholder who is reviewing an investment report," Liam noted. "It's all about ensuring the reader of the data has the proper context to **focus on the results** generated."

"Let's move on to 'Communicate,'" Liam said.

"**Communication** may be the most important element," Warren added.

"That's for sure," Liam agreed. "Everything fails without consistent communication. An organization must get in the habit of regularly communicating results to various stakeholders. This could mean an annual report for the average donor, a special report at a President's Weekend for significant ministry partners, or a carefully constructed in-depth performance report for the investment committee. Consistent communication is vital, both in good times and in more challenging environments! Ongoing communication achieves two major objectives: it builds stakeholder trust and demonstrates an ongoing commitment to transparency. This enhances stakeholder commitment."

"Stakeholders don't just want to hear from you in the good times," Warren chimed in. "They also want to know when things aren't going well. This may seem counterintuitive, but stakeholders will trust you more and be aware of when the organization needs additional support if you keep them in the communication loop."

"I think that is true," Doug echoed. "I know one of the things I have most appreciated about Tom and Koen at Chrysalis is their willingness to be honest when the organization has experienced hard times. As a board member and key stakeholder, I feel connected and valued as a partner. When I see the good news and the bad, I see Chrysalis is not just after my money when they are short on funds."

"You've clearly got this reporting element down, Doug," Liam smiled. "FAC will work with Chrysalis's internal team as much as necessary to help develop relevant reports for the investment committee."

"Great," Doug said, "Koen and Tom have already developed solid internal and external reporting for the board and for our other key stakeholders. For example, I love Chrysalis's annual report because it uses pictures to communicate impact, but other reports need to focus on the numbers. We've developed a great set of financial reports that we utilize with the finance and audit committee. We need your help to develop appropriate reporting for our growing gift annuity pool, donor advised fund platform, charitable trusts, and any other gift arrangements we are willing to accept. I'm sure you'll work with Jim on that."

"We certainly will!" Warren was enthusiastic. "You know, Doug, we have accomplished so much today! I'm thrilled to see Chrysalis taking these steps. We are grateful to be a part of the team, and we can't wait to see how the organization grows as you continue along the 'worthiness continuum.'"

"Yep," Doug laughed. "This is the next step along that continuum. Koen will be thrilled! We've put together an investment committee, built out our investment philosophy, constructed a plan to complete the relevant investment policy documents, and begun work on a reporting structure that will allow us to monitor the investment program and provide results to key stakeholders. Thanks for the help in moving us forward. I can't wait to report our progress back to Jim, Tom, and Koen, and let them know we're moving along the continuum!"

Waving goodbye, Doug headed home. Feeling good about the day's accomplishments, Liam and Warren collected their materials and set about outlining next steps for the FAC team.

CELEBRATION

"Hey, Jim!" Mary Pat Kingston exclaimed. Jim snapped back to the present with a jolt.

"Hey, Mary Pat," Jim smiled warmly. Shortly after he joined the team, Koen introduced him to Mary Pat. A special relationship had grown between them, maturing throughout his 20-year tenure at Chrysalis.

"So, what's the big news?" Mary Pat asked. She had bright blue eyes undimmed by her nearly 85 years and enough energy for a woman half her age. She eyed Jim carefully. "What's that man got up his sleeve this time?"

She poked Jim in the chest. "You never know with Koen," she said.

"I don't know, Mary Pat," Jim replied truthfully.

"What do you mean, you don't know?" Mary Pat insisted. "I've been to all ten of these President's Weekends, and I've never heard of such a thing. What's the big secret?"

"I don't know," Jim said again, just a bit uncomfortably. "Koen hasn't filled me in yet either."

"Hmph!" Mary Pat grunted. "Well, I sure hope it's good news! After 2008 and the challenges of the last few years, I'm ready for something positive."

"I sure hope so, too, Mary Pat," Jim said. "We've been through a tough few years, and we certainly appreciate your partnership during that time!"

"You know me, Jim." Mary Pat beamed. "I've been all in ever since Koen dug us out of that terrible spot years ago."

Jim smiled, "You've truly been a champion for Chrysalis, Mary Pat. We couldn't do it without you!"

"Oh, yes, you could," she laughed. "I'm just a little fish, Jim, and you know it. But God's allowed me to help Chrysalis out. You're right. I do believe in what we're doing, and I am thrilled to be a small part of His bigger plan!"

As Mary Pat headed off to the next session, Jim wondered again what Koen was going to announce at the conference. He had been hinting to Jim for weeks about some exciting information he planned to reveal at the President's Weekend.

Mary Pat had been engaged with Chrysalis from the beginning of Koen's tenure. She had both watched and participated as Koen pulled Chrysalis back from the brink and began the journey to financial freedom. Chrysalis made significant strides under Koen's leadership. The organization paid off its debt, and, with Tom's help, right-sized its expense load. Koen initiated a new strategic plan and outlined his long-term strategy. He wanted Chrysalis to continue to grow its worldwide missional footprint, and that meant more boots on the ground. Achieving that objective meant increased missional support, but Koen also wanted to build a 50-million-dollar endowment to help offset the administrative overhead paid by their missional field staff. This approach made it easier for Chrysalis to attract field staff.

Chrysalis could not achieve Koen's goal with its existing donor base. They needed a new approach, and donors like Mary Pat helped Jim and Koen discover how to begin the journey. Jim smiled to himself. It was, he thought, the next step on Koen's **worthiness** continuum. Jim wiped a tear from his eye as he watched Mary Pat stop to talk with another long-time donor. He realized how much he admired her drive, determination, and sense of stewardship. Without Mary Pat and others like her, Chrysalis would have continued to flounder. As he looked around the room at so many familiar faces, Jim reflected on the effort it had taken to build and maintain these important relationships.

PERSONAL WORTHINESS

Following Doug's meeting with FAC, Chrysalis's investment committee finalized its investment philosophy, approved investment policies for each pool of Chrysalis's assets, and developed a reporting procedure to keep stakeholders apprised of results. The committee would continue to monitor all invested assets and report regularly to the Chrysalis board. They had worked with the finance team, the board, and the investment committee to put in place the necessary components related to organizational worthiness! Now, the team could articulate Chrysalis's vision and mission accurately and succinctly.

Chrysalis was a member of ECFA and participated in an annual audit. The organization maintained internal controls and procedures to direct and secure funds dedicated to fulfilling the vision. The finance team and the development team worked together to create a policy outlining what types of gifts Chrysalis would accept, along with a plan for addressing exceptions to that policy.

Chrysalis's management team and the board worked together to set up an investment committee to oversee funds entrusted to the organization. The investment committee hired a skilled investment consultant to assist in the development of investment philosophy, investment policies, and the management and administration of the Chrysalis investment program.

Finally, the investment committee, the consultant, and Chrysalis's management team worked together to put in place a reporting structure that kept stakeholders abreast of the financial well-being of the organization. The reporting structure also designated an appropriate level of information and transparency around the various gift arrangements for which Chrysalis was responsible. The completion of these tasks and the committee's acceptance of its oversight role meant that Jim could move further along the worthiness continuum.

A couple of months later, Jim sat across the table from John Reese and April Johnson. John was Chrysalis's new major donor development officer, and April was Jim's right hand. April not only handled Jim's administrative needs, but she also directly supported Jim's development efforts with donors. Together, Jim, John, April, and Koen were responsible for donor development and fundraising efforts at Chrysalis. Jim and April had been working together for a couple of years, and John had recently joined their team to assist Jim in building out Chrysalis's major donor development program. John, a veteran consultant with KPMG, was a sharp dresser with reading glasses, blue eyes, and an energetic manner.

"Personal worthiness, that's the key," Jim stated emphatically. John and April looked at him blankly.

"Jim," John began, polishing his glasses while he looked across the table. "I've heard you and Koen talk about the worthiness continuum. Now that I've been at Chrysalis for a few months,

I can clearly see all the work that the organization has put into organizational worthiness, but honestly, I have no idea what you're talking about! Personal worthiness, what is that?"

April agreed, "I've been with you for a few years now, and I don't think I've ever heard you refer to personal worthiness!"

Jim smiled, "Well, maybe I haven't really referred to it that way. After listening to Koen for the last several years and working together to enhance Chrysalis's organizational worthiness, I've realized that the next step along Koen's worthiness continuum is personal worthiness."

"What's that?" Koen asked, his head in the doorway. "I was walking by the conference room, and I thought I heard my name."

"Come on in if you've got a minute," Jim said. "We were just talking about worthiness."

"Worthiness!" Koen repeated, "I thought organizational worthiness was my topic." He grinned.

"It is, it is," Jim laughed, "but like you are always saying, we must keep moving Chrysalis along the worthiness continuum. I've realized we have much further to go!"

"We do?" Koen looked puzzled.

"Yes," Jim replied, "We not only have to be **organizationally worthy**, but we also have to be **personally worthy**."

> We not only have to be organizationally worthy, but we also have to be personally worthy.

"That sounds intriguing," Koen said, grabbing a chair. "Can I join you?"

"Of course," Jim said, "we would love to have you. I must warn you, I haven't worked out all of the details yet."

"Oh? You sounded pretty sure of yourself before Koen walked in," April teased.

Jim laughed, "Well, honestly, I am still working it all out! But in the last several years of working with donors, I've realized something."

"What's that?" John asked.

"Well, organizational worthiness is incredibly important. People need to be able to trust the organization they support with their funds. They need to believe that the organization will steward those funds well and will utilize them efficiently to achieve the mission and ultimately fulfill the vision of the organization. It is also true that people give to people. Donors will only give a truly transformational gift to people they trust," Jim continued. "Donors may love the mission and vision of an organization, and they may recognize that the organization is worthy of their gift. Ultimately, they will only consign that gift to a person they trust. The individual asking for the funds must elicit trust from the donor!"

"I see," April said excitedly, "it is not enough for the donor to trust the organization. They must trust us, too."

"Exactly," Jim said. "The donor needs to believe we are competent and have their best interests at heart. They need to know we understand biblical stewardship. Like I said, I don't have it all worked out yet, but I think the first step toward personal worthiness is related to stewardship.

You see, as I have been working with Chrysalis's donors over the last few years, I have realized I can't ask others to do what I haven't done myself."

PHILOSOPHY OF STEWARDSHIP

John still looked a little uncertain. "I'm still not sure I understand," he said.

"Well, if I am going to ask other people to give their time, talents, and treasure to Chrysalis, if I am going to advise them as a steward, then I need to develop my own philosophy of stewardship. If I don't have a plan for my own giving, if I haven't developed a heart of generosity, how can I ask someone else to give?" Jim asked.

Koen blinked in surprise. "Why didn't I think of that!" he exclaimed. "Jim, this is brilliant. I completely agree. I can't build trust with a donor by asking them to do something I'm not willing to do myself. That would be disingenuous!"

Always the practical one, John asked, "So, how do we go about doing this, Jim? I mean, I believe I am a generous guy. I give money to charity, and I try to be a good steward, but what you are describing sounds like more than a financial commitment. What else do I need to do?"

"John, I'm hoping we can figure out what it means together." Jim spoke thoughtfully, "I've begun to develop my own 'philosophy of stewardship,' but I also recognize that it's easy to have blind spots when it comes to generosity. I want to be generous and a good steward of what God has entrusted to me, but I think we all need help in living out our faith in this way."

Jim continued, "We've all been given gifts from God to steward. Before you can tell someone else the best way to steward the gifts they have been given for God's glory and the advancement of His Kingdom, you must know yourself. Your personal stewardship philosophy involves answering the very questions you are asking donors to answer because giving is spiritual before it is mechanical. As I've worked on my own philosophy of stewardship, I've thought of a few questions, but I thought it might be good to do a little brainstorming together. In fact, each of us around this table has, I'm sure, considered our stewardship responsibility before God. But we've probably never really written it down or considered the internal questions we need to ask ourselves or our donors. Between the four of us, I'm sure we can come up with some great questions!"

"What you're saying really resonates with me, Jim. I've thought about these kinds of things as I've talked to donors, but I'll be honest, I'm a little embarrassed I haven't thought about it for myself in the same way. I love your idea of coming up with questions. I'll be the scribe," Koen joked, heading to the whiteboard.

There were a few minutes of awkward silence, as each person around the table considered what they were being asked to do. Jim sat in the silence, praying that God would lead the discussion.

Finally, breaking the silence, April threw out the first question. "What has God given you to give away?"

"Great, April." Koen wrote that down.

"How about, 'Where do you want to go with your time, talent, and treasure?'" John asked. Both Jim and April nodded as Koen wrote the question on the board.

"One question my wife and I have been wrestling with is, 'How much is enough to give?' I think that question is hard as we look at our kids and grandkids. It's easy to get distracted by the fun of giving to them, but I don't think generosity should just bless my family. That's not sacrificial, is it?" Jim pondered.

April responded, "So, are you saying giving can't be fun?"

Jim looked thoughtful. Koen jumped in, "No, I think it can be fun to give, even sacrificially, but I think Jim is trying to push us a bit to think beyond what is easy. Is that right, Jim?"

"Yeah, I think so. I guess I just want to think beyond me and even my community. I'm trying to figure out what it looks like to pursue Kingdom impact," Jim said.

John shared, "So, then another question might be, 'Where and how do your investments have the most impact?'"

"When it comes to giving generously, how much consideration do I give to my family?"

"How does my giving reflect my faith?"

They were all throwing out questions now.

"Slow down, slow down. I'm not the best with a dry-erase marker!" Koen struggled to keep up as John, April, and Jim peppered him with questions.

"Can I use my giving to impact the faith of my children?"

"Wow, that's a great one, John," Koen said, furiously writing.

"How can my giving grow my faith?"

"Okay, so I'm going to wrap us up with a question I always ask donors, 'How does the organization's vision link to your own personal vision for giving?'" Koen wrote this last question as the verbal barrage wound down. He stood back to admire his handiwork.

"Guys, this is great," Jim exclaimed as he read through the completed list. "I'm sure there are additional questions that we could add or that a donor might think of on their own, but this is a really solid start!"

Koen sat back down, and they all studied the board. April voiced what they all were thinking, "These are great questions, but where do we go from here?"

"Well," Jim said, "I've been thinking about personal worthiness for a while, but this discussion has really helped me think about it in a new way. I wonder about sharing these questions with our donors, but first, I think we have to share them with the other members of our team. Could we include these questions in a form that our team at Chrysalis could complete?"

Koen replied, "I love that idea of creating a personal 'Philosophy of Stewardship.' In fact, I would love to share it with the larger organization."

Jim replied, "Like I said, I've been working on my own philosophy of stewardship. This brainstorming session has helped solidify many of the important questions. I think it is a great idea to share it. We can each complete our own individualized philosophy. Then we can begin using these questions with our donors to help them determine their own philosophy of stewardship. I've found that some donors already have these issues figured out, but others haven't really thought about these questions. This methodology will help them clarify their giving objectives.

"What we really want to do," Jim continued, "is help our donors clarify their role as stewards and, at the same time, clarify what they are passionate about. If we can align the donor's passion for giving with the vision and mission of our organization, we create an extremely compelling reason to give!"

"I think I'm beginning to see how this works," John said. "If a donor is passionate about feeding the hungry, I can help them see how Chrysalis's mission for providing food to those displaced by armed conflict aligns with that passion."

"Or, if my donor is really excited about sharing Christ's love with the suffering, then I can highlight our missional focus!" April chimed in.

"Exactly," Jim said. "As we begin to dig deeper into our donors' philosophies of giving, we can help them uncover what they are truly passionate about and help them align those passions with opportunities to give!"

"Wow, Jim," Koen was enthusiastic. "Having a philosophy of stewardship is clearly important for anyone in development. Do you think there are other elements that tie into the development of a personal philosophy of stewardship for us here at Chrysalis?"

Jim thought for a moment. "You know," he said, "this is really part of our role in helping our donors be good stewards of what God has entrusted to them. But to help them do that, we must build trust in our relationship so we can cover their vulnerability as they share answers to these personal questions. This kind of relationship really relies on two components I have decided to refer to as 'continuity' and 'care.' I want our Chrysalis team to exhibit these qualities. I know there will always be turnover in our organization. As much as possible, I want one person to work with a donor on an ongoing basis so they can really build a relationship with that donor. Secondly, I want this one person to focus on caring for their donor. In my mind, caring for the donor means we get out to see them in person regularly, we look out for their best interests even if that doesn't immediately help Chrysalis, and we provide sound advice. That last point means our team needs to be knowledgeable and have a good support system."

"This concept of personal worthiness really does seem like the next step on the worthiness continuum! I can't wait to see how you and the team leverage these questions and concepts in your donor meetings," Koen said. "I certainly plan to use it in mine. I'm sure there are other ways that personal worthiness plays into our donor relationships as well."

Jim, John, and April finalized the personal philosophy of stewardship form and agreed that, to the greatest extent possible, they would apply Jim's standards of care and continuity to all Chrysalis donor relationships. Along with the form, April created a document outlining what the Chrysalis stewardship department meant by care and continuity. This document became part of Chrysalis's training package for all new fundraising team members.

Each new team member had to develop their own philosophy of stewardship and agree to exercise the Chrysalis standards of care and continuity to the best of their ability.

CELEBRATION

That meeting, Jim thought, was really the first time he had begun to articulate what personal worthiness looked like and how he was beginning to use it to build Chrysalis's donor base. He, John, April, and Koen had all clarified their own individual philosophies of stewardship, and as a result, they each realized that their work was a calling! They were called to help donors steward the assets entrusted to them. Part of this stewardship calling required them to build deeper relationships with donors. Those deeper, more trusting relationships led to stewardship conversations. As he looked around the room at this tenth President's gathering, Jim realized that many of the people in the room were people that he, Koen, April, or John had built deep and lasting relationships with over the years. Sure, some of those in the room were brand new relationships. Some, like Mary Pat, went back even further. Most of Chrysalis's major donors could be traced back to Chrysalis's initial commitment to build deeper relationships, relying on the standards of care and continuity, and utilizing the philosophy of stewardship questions to help discover a donor's passion and stewardship responsibility.

As Jim studied the donors around the room, he laughed to himself. His knowledge of gift strategy had come quite a long way, too. Personal growth was an important part of personal worthiness as well! Some of the folks in the room wouldn't be there today if one of the Chrysalis team had not been able to help determine which gifting strategy would work best for the donor. George Owens, over there in the corner talking to Christina Delaney, might never have become a significant donor if April hadn't explained to him how a donor advised fund worked. Jim grinned to himself as he thought back to that time several years ago when April finally found a solution that bridged George's passion for giving with a strategy that achieved his goals after months of asking questions and long discussions.

DONOR ADVISED FUNDS

Jim could hear April on the phone in her office. "I understand, Mr. Owens," she said politely. "It is certainly difficult to pull all the receipts together for your accountant. Yes, I know supporting the missionaries is more important than the tax break, but as a steward, you want to take advantage of the tax code as much as you can! You know, Mr. Owens," April continued, "if you have a few minutes, maybe I could explain a strategy to you that could help alleviate the challenge of documenting all your gifts to different organizations." April paused. "Is that something you would be interested in learning more about?

"What was that?" she asked. "Oh, you would like to hear about it. Great! Well, let me try to explain. You see, you could utilize a donor advised fund account. A donor advised fund, or a DAF, is kind of like your own charitable giving account. You can contribute cash, securities, real property, or even a business interest to your donor advised fund and receive an immediate deduction. You see, your contribution to the donor advised fund is an immediate contribution to charity. You are giving up ownership of your asset to the charity in return for an immediate deduction. There are a few exceptions for unique types of assets, but in most cases, you will receive a deduction for the full fair market value of your gift when you contribute.

"However," April continued, "in most cases, the assets are liquidated, and the funds are held in a donor advised fund account. That's right, Mr. Owens, Chrysalis will hold the donor advised fund account in your name. With a donor advised fund, you retain the right to advise us regarding when to make gifts and to which charities. As long as the mission of those charities is not antithetical to the mission of Chrysalis, we will process the gift on your behalf!"

"The nice thing is," April said, "you only receive one receipt from us here at Chrysalis. We make those other gifts for you, but you only have to keep track of the one receipt. Yes, sir, that's right. You can make gifts out of that account on an ongoing basis, but you receive one receipt for the amount you contribute to the account." She paused again as he spoke.

"Oh, yes," April answered, "you can continue to make new contributions whenever you want, and each one is tax-deductible.

"What's that?" she asked. "Oh, of course, sir. You can make a gift of stock one time and a gift of cash the next.

We are happy to facilitate this type of arrangement for you, even if not all the money is going to Chrysalis."

Jim remembered it had been this conversation which led to George Owens setting up a donor advised fund account with Chrysalis. Over the next several years, George had contributed publicly traded stock, cash, and even real estate to his donor advised fund. The creation of a DAF simplified George's giving and allowed him to support several charities, including Chrysalis, which he was passionate about. Jim's ongoing interactions with George through George's donor advised fund led to a stronger relationship and a deeper engagement with Chrysalis.

As Jim reflected on George's partnership with Chrysalis, he realized that with each gift to the DAF, George's engagement with Chrysalis deepened. As George's relationship with Jim and Chrysalis deepened, George became more and more engaged with the organization. Now, he was one of Chrysalis's most significant donors. This was not only true of George, Jim realized. As he looked around the room, Jim recognized face after face. Donors who, through various gift arrangements, had deepened and solidified their commitment to Chrysalis. As he finished up his last cup of coffee, Jim wondered if he could pick out a donor for each unique gift arrangement Chrysalis offered. It was kind of crazy, he thought. Like each donor, each gift arrangement had a story to go along with it.

THE BEQUEST

There was Christina Delaney. Jim first noticed her talking to George. Jim remembered that about ten years ago, he was on a trip to the Midwest to meet with some Chrysalis donors, and he stopped to see Christina. At that point, Christina had been a solid, mid-level donor to Chrysalis for a number of years. Jim offered to take her out for coffee and share a bit more about the impact Chrysalis was making around the world. Christina jumped at the chance to get together, he remembered. Jim had been a bit surprised at her willingness, but when they met at the coffee shop, he learned that Christina's husband had died unexpectedly of a heart attack earlier that year. Christina was grappling with the reality of death and what would happen to her assets when she passed away. While she wanted the bulk of her assets to go to her two children, she wondered if there was a way for her to continue to help Chrysalis after she died.

Jim explained that she could include Chrysalis as a beneficiary in her will. She could leave funds to the organization the same way she would leave funds to her family.

Christina was thrilled! She believed strongly in the work Chrysalis was doing around the world. By naming Chrysalis in her will, she could continue to support that work long after she was gone. In fact, as she talked with Jim, she realized she could do more in death for the ministry than she had done in life!

Now, Jim thought as he looked at her fondly from across the room, since she had redone her will, Christina had become even more committed to her current support of Chrysalis. Continued engagement with Jim and with the organization led to a deeper connection, and now Christina was a significant donor.

The Gift Annuity

Across the room, Jim noticed Don Chapman talking with Sam Ortland. *Don's a great guy!* Jim thought. He remembered meeting Don eight or nine years ago at a fundraiser dinner Koen hosted in St. Louis.

Don was an engineer, conservative, detailed, and precise. He and Jim sat together at dinner that evening, and Jim learned a great deal about Don's passion for engineering. It was this passion, Don said, that led him to Chrysalis. Don worked for a global engineering firm, and his firm was engaged in a project in Sudan. While he was on site facilitating the project, he encountered a Chrysalis team working with South Sudanese displaced by the conflict. He was impressed with the efforts of the Chrysalis team. After some quick background research on Chrysalis, Don started giving regularly.

He shared all of this with Jim as they ate, and at the conclusion of the meal, Don indicated he would like to do more to support the organization. He casually mentioned that he was thinking of giving an additional gift when his next CD matured. Jim asked about the CD, and Don shared that it was part of his overall retirement plan. He could not give away the entire CD, he noted. He needed the bulk of the principal for retirement, but he felt he could give part of the money in a current gift to Chrysalis.

Jim thanked him profusely for his heart of generosity and went on to ask if Don had ever considered a gift annuity?

"A gift annuity?" Don asked, "What is that?"

"Well, it's similar to a commercial annuity," Jim explained, "but with a gift component. You exchange the cash from your CD redemption for an annuity with Chrysalis. In its simplest form, the annuity then pays you income for life. At your death, the remaining portion of the original principal becomes a gift to Chrysalis. You receive an immediate tax deduction for the present value of that future gift to charity. A gift annuity could potentially be a great solution for you, Don," Jim explained.

"Wow, what a cool concept!" Don was clearly energized by the plan. "This strategy would allow me to make a larger gift to Chrysalis and meet my retirement objectives at the same time. I could still make my current gift as well?" Don asked.

"Absolutely," Jim replied. "Whatever amount you want to give when your CD matures, we can take the amount you want to give when your CD matures as a current gift, and then fund a gift annuity with the remainder of the proceeds."

"I love this idea!" Don said.

Don was pleased, and that initial annuity led to a deeper relationship. Now, eight or nine years later, Don had initiated several gift annuities with Chrysalis and was more involved than ever. The initial conversation led to a current gift and the funding of an annuity, and it also led to greater engagement on Don's part.

THE CHARITABLE TRUST

Many donor relationships were like that, Jim thought. They took time and effort to develop, but, ultimately, they resulted in significant gifts to the organization both now and in the future. In fact, the guy talking to Don, Sam Ortland, was another great example!

Sam was a significant Chrysalis donor. With retirement looming, he was preparing to sell a highly appreciated piece of real estate. After reading an article on Chrysalis's website that mentioned asset-based giving, Sam reached out to Jim to learn more.

Sam shared that he wanted to get out of the day-to-day management of the rental property, but he needed income to replace the lost rent. When Sam sold the property, the capital gains taxes were going to significantly reduce the amount he could reinvest.

Jim introduced the concept of a charitable trust. He explained to Sam that he could gift his rental property to the trust before the sale, and then the property would be sold by the trustee of the trust. Because the trust was a charitable vehicle, it would avoid paying capital gains on the sale of the funding asset. The proceeds could then be invested in a diversified portfolio to produce income for Sam in retirement. This strategy would result in an immediate deduction for Sam, allow him to avoid paying capital gains on the sale of his rental property, and produce an income that he could utilize to help fund his retirement. At Sam's death, any remaining assets in the trust would be gifted to Chrysalis.

Sam was intrigued by the strategy. He and Jim worked carefully through the details to ensure Sam fully understood the irrevocable nature of this type of gift. Ultimately, they determined that a charitable trust was a great solution for Sam and his family. With the blessing of Sam's long-time accountant, they moved forward. The result was a two-million-dollar trust with Chrysalis as the trustee. Liam's team at FAC facilitated the ongoing management of the trust, prepared the tax return and K-1 each year, and took care of the quarterly income distributions that went back to Sam.

Sam continued to receive income from the trust, and Jim talked with Sam often, but not just about the trust. Their relationship was actually very sweet. Sam had become a dear friend as they shared details about life—vacations, news about the kids—and Sam had become a mentor as he shared with Jim some of the challenges of retirement.

The trust had been a vehicle that deepened Sam's commitment to Chrysalis, leading to additional current giving and connecting him with other parts of the organization, the investment committee, FAC, and the donor development team. The trust had been a great success, and Jim was grateful that his job had allowed him to know Sam.

The Pooled Income Fund

The Whites, Jim noticed, were just heading out the door. Theirs was an interesting story, he thought. They might never have become Chrysalis donors at all, but a few years ago, some mutual friends of Chrysalis, the Scotts, heard Chad and Olivia White's company was having a fantastic year. They were at dinner together when the topic came up. Both Chad and Olivia were excited, of course, but they also mentioned that the banner year was likely to bring along with it a pretty significant tax hit.

"You should talk to our friend Jim," Elisa Scott said.

"He's helped Fred and me with several challenging tax situations."

"Is he an accountant?" Olivia asked Elisa.

Jim grinned at the thought!

"No!" Elisa laughed. "He's actually a fundraising guy who works with a ministry we support."

"A fundraiser?" Olivia was puzzled. "What can he do to help? We have an accountant and a tax attorney."

"I just think it's worth a conversation," Elisa said.

"Yeah," her husband Fred chimed in. "Jim's got all kinds of good ideas when it comes to creative tax solutions. Of course, most of them involve some sort of charitable gift."

"Well, I think I would rather make a gift than pay all those taxes," Olivia's husband Chad remarked.

That conversation led to an initial phone call with Jim, and then to a face-to-face meeting. Jim remembered that meeting well. He met Chad and Oliva near their home at a coffee shop on a bright, cold November day. Chad and Olivia had come through the door together. Chad was a big, bluff Midwesterner, and Olivia was sweet, blonde, and sharp as a tack.

"You must be Jim," Chad thundered as he crushed Jim's hand in his massive paw. "I'm Chad, and this is my wife, Olivia. Fred and Elisa have told us all about you. They said you could solve all our problems!" Chad grinned.

"Don't mind him, Jim," Olivia said quietly, "Thanks for taking the time to meet with us."

"My pleasure," Jim laughed, "I don't know about solving all your problems, though. I'll certainly give it my best shot! Let me get you some coffee."

They ordered, and Jim led the way to a table near the wall in the back. He helped Olivia to a chair and then sat with his back to the wall.

"It's the old Texas gunfighter instincts," Jim joked, "I always sit with my back to the wall when I can!" Chad and Olivia laughed. "You mentioned when you called that Fred and Elisa suggested you contact me."

"Yes," Chad said, and looked inquiringly at Olivia. She nodded slightly, and Chad continued, "You see, Jim, Olivia and I run a small architectural design firm, and we have had a particularly good year. Our personal income this year will be nearly a million dollars more than it was last year, and we are going to get hit hard with income tax. Our accountant tells us that between state and federal taxes, we'll owe nearly $500,000."

"We've already maxed out our retirement options," Olivia added. "And it doesn't seem like our accountant thinks there is much more we can do."

"Have you considered any type of charitable giving strategy?" Jim asked.

"Well, we always give to our church, and we gave to a couple of other charities this year," Chad replied. "You know, we really need to squirrel away some of this money for the future," he added. "We aren't getting any younger!"

Jim chuckled. "Isn't that the truth? Age catches up with all of us! Have you ever heard of a pooled income fund?"

"Nope, can't say I have," Chad answered. "Tell us about it."

"Well, a pooled income fund, or PIF, is a unique gifting device that can, in certain economic environments, provide a high current deduction, but also distribute some income back to the donors for their lifetime." Jim stopped to be sure that Chad and Olivia were tracking with him.

"That sounds intriguing," Olivia said. She was clearly following the conversation carefully.

"If we set up a new PIF, we get to use the last three years' prevailing low interest rates to calculate the deduction," Jim continued. "So, if the two of you set up a new PIF with Chrysalis, the deduction is likely to be around 70 percent of the amount you contribute to the PIF. Based on the investment policy for the PIF, you could receive three to four percent in income for the remainder of your life. It's also possible that if interest rates go up in the future or if we build in some unique language surrounding capital gains, we could potentially distribute to you at an even higher rate. Based on the 50 percent tax rate you mentioned, this strategy would create a deduction for you of approximately $350,000 on that gift of $500,000 and should result in tax savings of approximately $175,000," Jim finished.

"Wow," Chad was stunned, "that sounds pretty attractive to me. Can we get the funding principal back if we need it?"

"No," Jim answered, "the gift to the PIF is irrevocable."

"Okay," Chad was thoughtful, "if we give the money to this, what did you call it, Jim, a pooled income fund, then we can't get the money back. Instead, we create a significant current deduction this year to help with our taxes. And we receive income for life, right?"

"Yep, that's about the size of it," Jim said.

"Why wouldn't our accountant have mentioned this?" Olivia wondered.

"I can't say for sure," Jim answered. "But remember, with a PIF you are making a gift, and perhaps your accountant was uncomfortable recommending that you give away money."

"We are making a gift," Chad agreed, "but we'll get the income over the years to come, which will provide a significant benefit to us during our retirement. It really feels like a win to me. We get to help people around the world through Chrysalis and, at the same time, support ourselves during retirement. Jim, this is great! We want to consider this strategy. What are the next steps we need to take?"

"We'll put together a proposal for you," Jim answered. "You can take that to your accountant and talk through it with him. If you need my help, I'm happy to chat with him. If necessary, we'll get our gifting specialists to walk him through the details."

They finished up the meeting, chatting about family, Chrysalis, and the coming Christmas season. Jim followed up with a proposal, and, after a call with the White's accountant, Chad and Olivia worked with Jim to get the PIF set up before the end of the year. That gift kicked off a relationship between Chad, Olivia, and Chrysalis. Jim connected with them regularly, and they became more and more engaged with the ministry as their relationship with Jim deepened and they learned more about the important work that Chrysalis was doing around the world.

THE CHARITABLE LEAD TRUST

Jim got up from the table to look for Ann. As he headed for the door, he caught sight of Roman Crandall leaving from the far side of the room. Roman's situation was unique, Jim thought. Roman inherited significant wealth. His family owned a multi-generational business, and, consequently, Roman's estate, including significant liquid assets, was taxable. Financially sophisticated, Roman employed several creative strategies to pass their wealth from one generation to the next.

Jim first met Roman at a major donor event Chrysalis held at Sea Island on the Georgia coast. Roman's family owned a place at Sea Island. Although he did not know much about Chrysalis, Roman had seen some information about the event at The Cloister and reached out to Chrysalis, expressing interest in their mission. John, from Chrysalis's major donor team, responded and quickly realized Roman's family represented significant financial capacity. John invited Roman and his wife, Melissa, to the President's Weekend that Chrysalis was hosting that year at The Cloister at Sea Island.

After hearing Jim introduce the concept of asset-based giving from the stage, Roman caught up with him later in the evening. They chatted over coffee, and then Roman got right to the point.

"Jim," he said, "I really like what Chrysalis is doing around the world. Many years ago, my family was forced to flee our ancestral home due to conflict. We immigrated to America, and my grandfather started our engineering business. As you know, the business has been successful. My wife and I have significant assets. I'm intrigued by Chrysalis's vision to offer hope to those displaced by armed conflict around the world, and I would like our family to be a part of that offering. Throughout this weekend, I have been impressed by Chrysalis's stewardship. We support many organizations, but few seem to really understand what enhanced organizational stewardship looks like. Clearly, Chrysalis gets it. This entire weekend has demonstrated how much you care about your financial partners, and you have done a great job outlining your standards for addressing concerns around the stewardship of funds entrusted to your care.

"It also seems to me," Roman continued, "that you actually know what you are talking about! We have a great estate planning attorney and several accountants, both personal and professional, but they are primarily concerned with helping us transfer wealth to our heirs with the smallest tax burden. That's important, of course, but I would like to find a way to do more philanthropically. You seem like the guy to help us accomplish this goal. I know we are new to the Chrysalis family, but I would like to sit down with you sometime and explore options to expand our charitable giving."

Jim remembered that initial meeting like it had just happened. The Crandall family was one of the wealthiest he had ever worked with, and that initial conversation led to multiple meetings. Over the course of the next year, Jim carefully reviewed both the Crandalls' estate planning documents and their assets. He and Roman discussed the family's wealth transfer strategy, their annual income, as well as their financial and philanthropic goals. Ultimately, they settled on an inter-vivos charitable lead annuity trust, or CLAT, funded with family-owned cash and corporate stock they wished to give to their children, estate tax-free.

Utilizing a charitable lead annuity trust allowed the Crandalls to transfer a significant amount of assets out of their estate with only a minimum amount of gift tax. At the same time, they were able to begin giving more to charity. The Crandalls funded their CLAT with $20,000,000.

They backed into a distribution rate that would zero out the estate tax and allow the remaining trust assets to go to the children after ten years. This was a huge win both for Chrysalis and for the Crandalls, Jim reflected. This endeavor was well worth the time and effort it had taken to work through the details and get the trust structured and funded.

CELEBRATION

The lunch ended, and most donors headed back inside for the early afternoon session. They were looking forward to hearing several Chrysalis partners share stories about the impact they were seeing from their ministry in war-torn areas around the world. Jim hurried to find Ann. They planned to attend this session together, and then they were going on a hike with a couple of donors with whom Jim was especially close.

Jim caught up with Ann on the veranda, and they headed in together. As they walked, Ann chattered on about the folks she had been talking with. "Jim," Ann tugged on his hand to get his attention, "are you even listening to me?"

"I'm trying," he grinned. "I just keep thinking about this news Koen is going to announce at the finale tonight."

"That's just what I was talking about," Ann sounded exasperated. "Everyone I run into is buzzing about it! I'm not sure Koen's ever been quite this mysterious. We all want to know what's happening."

"Well," Jim said, "I guess we'll just have to wait for tonight. It's not any easier for me, you know!" he laughed. "I'm just the development guy! I don't know everything."

"You must have some idea." Ann was sure Jim was holding out on her.

"No, honey, I really don't know what Koen plans to announce. As far as I know, we're on track for the year, although we're counting on some major gifts from this weekend to hit our final fundraising goals. It must be something more significant than that."

"Well, be ready." Ann pulled him into the large ballroom for the final session of the afternoon. "I'm sure the Whites and the Scotts will want to talk about it on our hike."

She waved at some friends across the room who had held seats for them and pulled Jim across the room. "Come on," she whispered, "they are ready to start!"

Jim followed her to the table, and they sat down with a group of friends from Chrysalis. However, as the first speaker began to talk about the impact Chrysalis was having in the Sudan, Jim once again found himself having a difficult time concentrating on the speaker. He couldn't seem to get his mind off the past!

He thought about how his own personal worthiness journey and growth laid the foundation for his relationships with the donors they planned to go hiking with after the session. Most likely, the Whites and the Scotts would never have become donors if Jim had not explored a growing knowledge about types of gift arrangements. There was much more to it than Jim originally thought.

THE TRUSTED GUIDE

As he reflected, Jim remembered a training event he'd held a few years back. Chrysalis's fundraising efforts continued to grow, and Jim realized his need for additional help. Koen, April, and John each contributed to the program in important ways, and Chrysalis's additional team members also helped to bolster fundraising efforts and support current relationships.

All the while, Jim and Koen consistently introduced new members to the worthiness continuum and walked them through the important aspects of organizational worthiness with the help of John and April. Even Tom participated. Jim smiled at the thought. In some ways, it had taken some time for Tom to buy into the elements of the worthiness continuum. Yes, he had been quick to support the idea of organizational worthiness, but convincing him to see the value in all the aspects of personal worthiness took some time.

However, Tom soon witnessed how the personal philosophy of stewardship impacted donors. After seeing the enormous benefit Chrysalis experienced due to increasingly complex gift arrangements, he, too, became a raving fan.

It wasn't the training, in and of itself, that caused the transformation, Jim thought. *But as I brainstormed with April, John, Koen, and Tom about what they wanted to teach, the epiphany came to us!*

Looking back, Jim remembered when Tom was talking about all the planned gifts the team developed. Almost midstream in his talk, Tom suddenly stopped and turned to Jim. "How do you sell those things anyway?" he demanded. "They seem complicated, and I've never figured out how you all convince one of our financial partners to use one of those vehicles! I mean, I understand how they work, and we have policies and procedures in place to be sure that the funds are protected and managed properly, but when the numbers are so big, how do you get donors to trust us?

"Of course, Liam's team over at FAC supports you and helps with both the structure and the management of the gifts. But how do you go about getting a donor committed to the concept?"

"Well, it's not selling, exactly," April said at first. But then she looked at Jim and laughed. "You know, I guess it really is selling, isn't it?"

"Yep!" Jim grinned. "It is selling, but you know, it's selling in a not-for-profit context!"

> It's selling in a not-for-profit context.

Koen started laughing. "Jim, you can't be serious! We aren't really selling these strategies to our ministry partners. I mean, you're helping them, and they're giving to Chrysalis. That doesn't really seem like a sale to me."

"That's the great thing about it," Jim exclaimed. "We are selling them on the mission, vision, and worthiness of Chrysalis."

"Well, when you put it that way," Koen surmised, "I guess you're right. That's what I do all the time. I mean, I'm so passionate about who we are and why we do what we do. I'm always happy to share with a prospective donor."

"I hear you," Tom broke in, "but I still don't see how personal worthiness results in a transformational gift like the charitable lead annuity trust the Crandalls set up or that last real estate gift the Scotts made."

The Model: Relate

"Huh," Jim paused. "You know, I never really thought about it quite like that, Tom." Jim thought for a moment, then headed to the whiteboard. "April, you're going to have to help me through this," he said as he grabbed a marker.

"It all begins with relationships," Jim said as he wrote, "Relationship," in big letters on the board.

"Yes," April chimed in. "First, we have to build a relationship with a prospective financial partner."

"That's the easy part," Koen reflected. "You reach out to someone for coffee or meet them at an event and begin to talk with them, get to know them. You learn about their life, family, what they're interested in, maybe even why they like Chrysalis. We talk about what interests them and what Chrysalis is all about."

Jim changed the word "Relationship" on the whiteboard to "Relate."

"Okay, people," he said, "to build a relationship with donors, we need to 'relate' to them. So, what are the most important elements of relating?"

Being Fully Present

"Being fully present is really important," April offered. "You know, when you sit down with someone, you really need to focus on them. You can't be distracted or thinking about what you want to say next. You need to fully engage."

"Absolutely," Koen agreed. "I've found I can't have my phone out, and most of the time I need to intentionally make eye contact so the other person knows I'm not only interested in what they are saying, but I am interested in them, you know, as a person. That means being interested in what they are interested in, and that I care about what is bothering them. If I can remain fully present, it lets the donor know I see them, not just their potential gift."

"They feel important, like they really matter," April continued.

Jim wrote, "Being fully present," on the whiteboard. "Great! I completely agree with that. And I have realized over the years it takes practice and intentionality to remain present with someone in the midst of deadlines, busy schedules, and wearable technology."

Tom laughed, "Is that why you don't wear a smart watch, Jim?" Blushing, Jim mumbled something about know-it-all CFOs who always have the last word. April and Koen were laughing, too.

Active Listening

"Okay, okay. Let's get back on topic," Jim tried to right the ship. "I believe the next key element is 'active listening.'"

Tom looked puzzled. "Active listening," he mused. "What's that?"

"It's closely related to being fully present," Jim said. "You must focus on what the person is saying, really seek to understand. Study them as a person while listening to the words they're saying. Remember, as much as 90 percent of communication is nonverbal, so paying attention to body language and making eye contact is often as important as the actual words spoken."

"It's like last night," April began, "my daughter was practically bouncing up and down as I came in the door. She started talking before I could even get the door closed 'Mom, I did it, I did it!' she shouted. 'Did what?' I asked. 'Duh. A round-off back handspring! I've only been trying to do it like every day for the last month.'"

"'That's so exciting,' I told her. 'I'm thrilled you were able to do it. It just took me a minute to catch up with you.' I couldn't help grinning. Her joy was infectious. She couldn't wait to tell her dad, and she bounced away before I could say anything else," April finished.

"That's a great example," Koen said. "Being present for your daughter allowed you to experience her joy in and passion for her sport. You could clearly see that accomplishing this move was important to her. You picked up on her excitement and were able to celebrate the moment with her."

Jim wrote, "Active listening," on the board. It's like being an active participant in the moment, he said. "Anything else?"

Common Interests

"You know, I've found looking for common interests has really served me well," Koen said. "Many times, as I've listened to a prospective ministry partner and engaged them in conversation, we find areas of common interest. This often gives me something to focus on in future conversations. You know I love football, golf..."

"Yes, and every other sport known to mankind!" April finished.

Koen grinned. "Well, you do have a point, April, but most people have a sport they're interested in, which helps me get the conversation rolling."

Jim added, "Look for common interests," to their list on the board.

"Okay, people," Tom said, "I can see how these elements are an important part of relating to anyone. Help me understand how they help in our partner development here at Chrysalis."

Creating a Safe Space

"Tom, please understand. Major donors don't have many people they can talk to about their financial situation. Think about it. If they say too much at church, people may treat them differently. If the financial environment is tough and they comment on how hard it is for their business, their employees may lose faith in them."

Jim was really warming to his theme now.

"Wealthy individuals need a safe place to talk about their financial situation, and we can provide that place. We're not too close, like a friend at church or work. Most of the time, our relationship is separate from their other circles of influence, and this gives them confidence in our ability to be discreet and maintain confidentiality. As we create this safe place and begin to build relational capital, we open the door to becoming a trusted advisor and confidant. We can be someone who can help in ways that are different from a financial advisor, a lawyer, or a pastor."

Knowing the Environment

"You know, I've found just a little knowledge of what's going on in the economy and markets can make a big difference in my connection with a potential financial partner," April said. "Knowing what's going on in their world allows me to better connect with them and build trust quickly. Like you said, Jim, I've found many of our financial partners don't have too many people they can talk to about their financial position. But they live and breathe this stuff. If the economy is falling apart, they are working on contingency plans for their business. If there's a debate about a potential new tax law that affects their estate planning situation, they're usually tuned in. I've found that if I'm aware of these, let's call them financial environmental issues, then it's easier for me to connect and build trust with donors."

"That's perfect, April. We need to be fully present, actively listen, look for common interests, and create a safe place for communication to happen. It really comes down to one key concept." Jim looked thoughtful. "The donor is the hero of our fundraising journey! I never really thought about it this way before. Our engagement with the donor can't simply be transactional! It is pastoral. We are called to be a steward to stewards. We help them on their journey of generosity, and we have the unique opportunity to be their trusted guide. But they are the hero of the story!"

Tom looked stunned. "I never thought of it that way."

"This is really powerful stuff," Koen said. "I mean, we have been engaging our financial partners this way for years, Jim, but I don't think we have ever really outlined our engagements this way before."

"No, I don't think we have. I guess I never followed this line of thinking quite this far." Jim seemed surprised as he looked at the whiteboard.

"Well, it is really helpful for me to think about it this way, but we still haven't gotten to the selling part yet," Tom said.

April grinned at Jim. "Tom's not letting that go, Jim.

You're going to have to give him more!"

The Model: Explore

Before Jim could answer, April said, "The next step in the process, Tom, is 'explore.'"

"What do you mean by explore?" Tom asked.

"Curiosity," Koen opined drily.

"Huh?" Tom's eyebrows rose.

"Oh, stop it!" April laughed. "What Koen's trying to say isn't all that mysterious, Tom." She looked at Koen, who tried to maintain his innocent expression. He, too, started laughing.

"We need to be curious about the donor's circumstances, that's all, Tom. We need to ask engaging exploratory questions. You know, draw them out," Koen continued. "I might ask something like, 'What is happening in your life at the moment?' or 'Can you tell me what business is like this year?' I want to get them talking about what's going on in their life. This is closely linked to our first step, relating. We must employ the skills we just outlined. We must be fully present and actively listen to what the person is saying."

Asking Engaging Questions

"There's another important skill in this phase of the process," April said.

"Oh, what's that?" Koen bantered back.

"Asking engaging questions!" April exclaimed.

"Asking questions is a skill?" Tom looked a bit skeptical.

"You bet it is. If you ask 'yes' or 'no' questions, you won't get very far! Be creative. There are some great books out there on the topic of asking questions," April said.

Jim wrote "Explore" and "Curiosity" on the board.

"You see, if you aren't careful, your conversation will never penetrate the surface. Let's say I'm driving home from school with my teenager in the car, and I ask a closed question like, 'How was your day?' What kind of answer am I going to get?" Jim asked.

"Fine!" Koen and April broke out in unison.

"Exactly. If I get creative instead, if I ask open-ended questions, I can take the conversation to a deeper, more meaningful place. If I'm not creative and I don't ask good questions, we'll never get past the basics," Jim finished.

Tom was nodding now. "I guess it makes sense.

Curiosity and open-ended questions lead you deeper into a positive relationship with the donor, and you begin talking about more meaningful things."

"Exactly. Opportunities flow from those more meaningful conversations. A donor or prospective financial partner may comment on how well their year is going at the business or mention a significant bonus."

"Or they could highlight a challenge they are having with a rental property," Koen offered. "Life change is another big one that often comes up. The family may be getting ready to move or adjusting to retirement."

"These are all significant events or circumstances we want to be alert to." April was refreshing her coffee and now turned to Tom. "You see, a deeper, more engaged conversation allows us to explore the donor's circumstances and leads to the next step in the process."

The Model: Find

"And that is?" Tom inquired obligingly.

"Find," Jim wrote on the board. "The next step is finding a problem."

"I don't get it." Tom looked at Jim blankly. "Why would we want to find a problem?"

April took the plunge. "It's all about creating dissonance, Tom. If I hear something significant in the conversation that may give me an opportunity to help the donor, I increase awareness of that element. I do this by creating dissonance, or identifying the problem. For example, if the donor mentions a large year-end bonus, I might say, 'Wow, that sounds great!' The donor might agree but then add, 'Yes, it is, but my taxes are going to be sky high because of it.'"

"Bingo, we've just uncovered a problem." Jim looked at Tom to see if he was following. Tom frowned.

"Maybe this example will help clarify things," Jim said. "If I'm having a conversation with a donor about retirement and they say they're going to need to sell some rental property, I need to be aware of any tax consequences associated with that transaction."

Jim continued to explain. "My knowledge is critical in both revealing the donor's problem and offering a helpful solution. Raising the issue of taxes is a way of creating dissonance or alerting the donor to a problem they may not have been anticipating."

The Model: Fix

"Yes, and when I do that, I often get the opportunity to move to the next step in the process, 'Fix,'" said Koen. The light dawned in Tom's eyes as Koen said the word "Fix."

"I get it!" Tom interrupted. "You make the donor aware of a problem they may be facing and offer them a charitable solution. Genius!"

The Model: Summary

"I'm glad you think so, Tom." Jim smiled. "I think so, too, and that is how we 'sell' in a not-for-profit context.

First, we relate to the donor. Then we explore with the donor by engaging them in a deep and meaningful conversation where we may find a point of dissonance, a problem the donor has not yet identified. We can then propose a solution to the problem through the use of a charitable vehicle like a donor advised fund, charitable gift annuity, pooled income fund, or charitable trust. When the donor accepts or agrees with our proposed solution, this is the point of closure in the sales process."

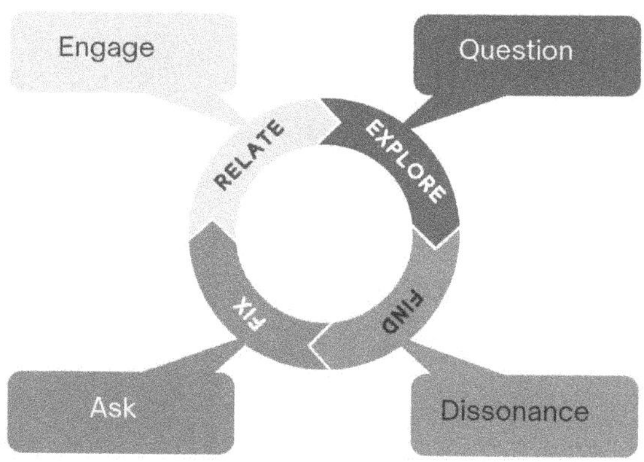

Tom shook his head as Jim wrote "Fix" on the whiteboard. "All these years, I've wondered how you, April, and Koen have successfully completed these major gift arrangements. Now I see how you've managed to do it.

Genius," he said again. "Why doesn't everyone use this model?"

Jim shrugged, "Lots of reasons, I suppose. It involves more time because you need to get to know the donor. The transactional framework can seem fast and simple. Using this model requires some knowledge. While you don't have to be an expert, you do need to know a little bit about charitable solutions, like how and when they should be used. Our approach requires emotional intelligence. We build relationships with people rather than just asking them for something we need. There are plenty of other reasons, but I suspect these are the most significant."

Jim sighed, "Unfortunately, many donors end up feeling like vending machines. They're asked to give to every new campaign, and it's easy for them to become disengaged, disenchanted, and disheartened by the whole process."

"That's certainly not what we want here at Chrysalis. Like you said earlier, Jim, we want the donor to be the hero of the story. We want to be the trusted guide helping them along their stewardship journey!" Koen walked to the board and thanked Jim. Then he turned to Tom, "Now do you see how this works, Tom?"

"It makes perfect sense," Tom agreed, "and I can really see how knowing and practicing these relational skills is essential to our fundraising success. It's another step along the worthiness continuum."

"Absolutely. Here at Chrysalis, selling in a not-for-profit context is synonymous with shepherding our donors along their stewardship journey. We begin by treating the donor as the hero of the story, building a relationship, and exploring their interests, passions, and objectives. Then we search for ways that we might be able to help them along that journey by identifying hidden problems or challenges. Finally, we propose charitable solutions as a potential solution for those tax and estate-related economic challenges we have identified."

CELEBRATION

As the speaker wrapped up the presentation on Chrysalis's impact in Sudan, Jim's mind snapped back to the present. He saw Fred Scott heading across the room toward him.

"Elisa's already headed back to the room to change clothes, so I hope we are still on for our hike," Fred said.

"Jim's been so preoccupied all day, I'm not sure he can actually walk!" Ann joked.

Jim laughed self-consciously. "I guess I have been a bit preoccupied today, but I'm definitely ready to get outside now."

The air outside the Ritz at Bachelor Gulch was crisp and inviting, and the gold leaves on the aspens beckoned as the couples all met up at the front of the hotel.

"This is such a beautiful setting," Olivia gushed. Elisa and Ann agreed as they headed up the well-marked path into the woods. The men followed along in companionable silence as they started up the trail.

"We've really enjoyed the event this year," Fred said. "Yeah, this place is amazing," Chad chimed in. "The content has been great, and Olivia and I have really enjoyed the speakers and hearing about the impact that Chrysalis is making around the world."

"We couldn't make this type of impact without friends like you," Jim said, walking along.

"I don't know about all that," Fred grinned back at Chad as he hopped over the small creek crossing the trail. "We're just small fish in a big pond."

"That's absolutely not true," Jim protested. "You and Olivia, Fred and Elisa, all of you are champions."

"Now that's what I like to hear!" Chad laughed. "I'm glad to know I'm a champion at something! It's certainly not running, at least not at my age in this mountain air. I'm already breathing hard, and this was supposed to be an easy hike." He looked pointedly at Jim.

"You're still a champion in my book, Chad," Jim said.

The path steepened, and the men hurried to catch up with their wives. They were too busy breathing to continue the conversation, but Jim's mind reached back to recall how the Whites and the Scotts had first become champions. It wasn't always that way, he remembered.

DONORS TO CHAMPIONS: DONOR

Jim's first contact with Fred and Elisa Scott was at a golf event. Fred and Elisa ended up in Jim's foursome.

"Here they are," Skip announced. "Jim, I want you to meet Fred and Elisa Scott. They're great folks, and they love to play golf!"

Fred, Elisa, and Jim all shook hands. "Skip and I play golf together all the time," Fred said. He mentioned you were having a charity tournament, and we figured Elisa could be our secret weapon."

Elisa grinned at Jim. "I'm not that good," she managed before both Skip and Fred interrupted.

"Don't let her kid you, Jim. She can really pound the ball!" Fred never missed an opportunity to brag about his wife's skill with a golf club.

"Elisa can ride with me," Skip said, "and that will give you and Fred an opportunity to get to know each other."

Jim and Fred climbed into their cart and headed out to the course.

"So, what's this ministry you're involved with?" Fred asked as they headed toward the first tee.

"Skip didn't tell you?" Jim shook his head in disbelief.

"Nope. Like I said, Skip and I play together all the time. This sounded like a fun day, so we jumped at the chance to get on the course. Tell me, Jim, what are you going to do with the proceeds from this tournament?"

"Chrysalis exists to offer the hope of Jesus Christ to those displaced by armed conflict around the world. We provide food, shelter, and the message of Christ's love."

"That sounds pretty cool." Fred was silent for a moment. "You know, Elisa and I are Christians, and I didn't even know Chrysalis existed. I'm thrilled to hear that our money will be put to good use."

Participation in the tournament involved a nice donation to Chrysalis, and Fred was so cavalier that Jim figured he wasn't really that interested in the ministry. While they played, neither Fred nor Elisa asked any other questions, and the golf game was pretty intense. So, when the event was over, Jim didn't expect much.

DONORS TO CHAMPIONS: INVESTOR

Jim sat down across the table from Fred. After their first round of golf, Jim stayed in touch. Fred and Elisa made a few additional small cash gifts to Chrysalis. Jim asked Fred to grab coffee so he could thank him for the most recent gift.

"So, Fred, how's Elisa doing?"

"Oh, she's fine. We're all doing fine, Jim." Fred seemed distracted and distant.

"Thanks for taking the time to meet with me. I want to thank you and Elisa for your recent gift to Chrysalis. As you know, this funding campaign will help advance our efforts in the Sudan and should allow us to support 2,000 additional displaced refugees."

"That's great, Jim," said Fred. "Elisa and I are happy to be a small part of what Chrysalis is doing in Africa. We really haven't been all that engaged, and I'm glad you took time out of your schedule to meet and fill us in. You know, I'm not sure I've ever had anyone from the organizations we support follow up with me personally."

Jim sipped his coffee. "Fred, we really are grateful for your involvement, and I would like to share more with you about what's new with Chrysalis. I was curious about you and Elisa. Skip introduced us, but I really don't know you well. Tell me more about your giving journey, what you're interested in, what seems exciting about Chrysalis."

Fred was quiet for a moment. "Elisa is very passionate about children," he finally said. "We haven't been able to have kids, and Elisa has always wanted children. When she saw those pictures of refugee kids, hurt by the war, losing their homes, stranded in another country, it just tore at her heartstrings. She really wants to help, and I guess," he looked at the table, "I just want to do whatever I can to support her in this."

He looked up at Jim, tears in his eyes. "You know, I can't control whether or not the Lord allows us to have kids, but I can help these little ones who are in such a bad place. I can help Elisa make an impact. I think both of us long to touch lives. Maybe this is an area where we can make a difference."

Stunned by Fred's vulnerability, Jim didn't know how to respond. They sat comfortably in silence for a few moments until Fred straightened up, clearing his throat.

"Gosh, Jim. I don't know what came over me. We hardly even know each other, and here I am unveiling my soul!"

Jim immediately recognized the mute appeal in Fred's words. He had experienced this before. Giving money was often connected to something deeper. Jim didn't rush to fill the silence, but he reached across the table and put his hand on the younger man's shoulder and looked him in the eye, seeking to convey care.

After a pause, he said, "First, I am so honored that you were willing to share with me. I know what it's like to long for something deeply, and I am deeply moved by your love for your wife."

Jim took a deep breath. "I know that we don't know each other well, but I want you to know that I am here because I care—even if you beat me at golf."

Fred smiled gratefully, "But you came here to talk to me about money, not about my problems."

Jim grinned. "I came to get to know you," he said, "and to thank you for your gift."

"You certainly got more than you bargained for," Fred chuckled. "I'm curious about how Chrysalis engages in these refugee camps."

They spent the next hour talking about Chrysalis's mission and work to provide shelter, food, and hope to families torn apart by war. By the end of the conversation, it was evident Fred was intrigued. "Jim, Elisa and I would like to get more involved. You mentioned this new initiative to impact an additional 2,000 refugees in Sudan. How much are you trying to raise to get this done?"

"Well, our short-term goal is a million dollars," Jim said. "We'll need more than that to continue supporting this particular refugee camp, but that will help the camp support the latest influx of refugees."

"Let me talk to Elisa." Fred finished his coffee and stood up. "I've got to head back to the office. Thanks for taking the time to get together."

"Absolutely. I wouldn't have missed it." Jim shook Fred's hand as they left the cafe and headed for his car.

Jim was surprised when, a week later, he got a note from Fred and Elisa with a significant check to help efforts in the Sudan. The note was in elegant script; Jim felt sure it was Elisa's hand. It read, "For the Children."

CELEBRATION

Jim was breathing hard. "An easy hike, they said," he muttered as he slogged along behind Ann. Ann and Elisa were chattering away. How do they have the energy to talk? He grinned ruefully to himself, thinking that his wife was rarely at a loss for words. He looked behind him. Fred was right on his heels, looking fresh as a daisy. Chad, on the other hand, was puffing like a steam engine and looked like he was about to pass out. "Hey, ladies," Jim called, "how about a short break? You're about to kill us old guys back here."

"You must be talking about Chad!" Olivia laughed. "He always looks like that when he's exerting himself."

"Like what?" Chad huffed as he caught up with the group.

"Like you're about to die, dear," Olivia said sweetly.

Chad grimaced. "Is that all the respect I get? Jim, I thought this was supposed to be an easy hike."

Ann blushed. "It's a bit harder than I expected," she said.

"For sure," Fred said, grinning. "I hope there is some reward at the end."

"The view is supposed to be stunning at the top," Ann said.

"I'm sure it will be worth it," Elisa said. Always the peacemaker, Elisa hated arguments.

"I don't think it's much farther," Ann said.

Jim rolled his eyes at Fred and Chad. "She always says that, and then she drags me a few hundred more miles."

The banter continued until Fred asked Jim in a more serious tone, "So, what's this big announcement of Koen's?"

Ann looked at Jim triumphantly. Jim rolled his eyes again and said, "Guys, I really don't know."

"What do you mean you don't know?" Chad demanded. "You must know."

"I really don't," Jim protested. "Whatever it is, Koen's kept it close to the vest."

"That's okay, Jim," Elisa said as she once again headed up the trail. "We'd better get moving so we can make it back in time for dinner and the celebration." The group trailed out behind Elisa with Jim bringing up the rear. Jim's thoughts turned once again to Fred and Elisa.

DONORS TO CHAMPIONS: PARTNER

Jim looked up from the menu to see Fred and Elisa walking up to the table. "Sorry, we're late, Jim." Fred looked embarrassed.

Jim stood up to shake Fred's hand and give Elisa a quick hug. "No problem at all!" he said, smiling.

"It's my fault," Elisa began. "I was chatting with a friend on the phone and lost track of time. Next thing I realized we needed to be leaving, and I wasn't ready!"

Jim laughed. "I've been married for a while myself, and I know how these things go. You gave me a chance to check out the menu and relax a moment."

Fred chuckled. "I'm starving. What looks good, Jim?"

"I'm leaning toward the New York strip," Jim said. "This place is known for its steaks, and I've been dying to try one. I'm so glad we could meet here tonight. I've been looking forward to it for weeks."

"We've been looking forward to this dinner, too," Elisa said. "Thanks for sending us that report detailing the impact that the ministry is having on the children. It just breaks my heart to think of those kids in such desperate situations, no place to call home, maybe missing parents, not enough to eat…," her voice trailed off.

"I know," Jim said gravely, "I think maybe the situation with the children is one of the toughest things we deal with."

The waiter came and took their orders. When they were settled in and waiting for their drinks, Jim continued, "Chrysalis works to protect those most vulnerable, and I think that is one of the most significant elements of our mission. We do that in several ways. First, whenever possible, we relocate them to an area outside the conflict. Second, we make sure they have access to clean water and food.

"If those basic needs are met, we seek to help resource and strengthen their family system. Often, the father has been taken from the family by the conflict, and we are working with mothers who have little education or training to provide for their families. Sometimes that means education or training, and sometimes that means providing economic opportunities. Our missionaries work with boots-on-the-ground organizations that help connect needs to resources. We can meet specific needs because we aren't dealing with a lot of red tape."

Elisa smiled a sad little smile. "I know Fred told you that we can't have any children. As I imagine being a single mother unable to provide for the basic needs of my child…," her words drifted off as tears fell from her eyes.

Fred reached for his wife's hand. His eyes pleaded with Jim, *What can we do? How can we play a more significant role?*

"Partner with us," Jim said. "Our work in Sudan is significant, and we would love for the two of you to engage more deeply. You connect with the heart of Chrysalis. You care for the 'least of these' in the same way we do. There's so much to do!

"You could join us on a trip to Sudan to see the kids," he continued. "We always need more hands, and it's a great opportunity to connect with what's happening on the ground."

Elisa was breathless as she looked at Fred. "Do you think we could go?"

"Why not?"

Again, Fred's eyes spoke volumes to Jim, as he continued, "I think that's a great idea. It will be an adventure." He chuckled, "Imagine the two of us traipsing through Sudan."

"We aren't exactly the roughing-it type, are we?" Elisa grinned. "I guess my little Coach purse and I will need to adjust, but I'm sure Jim can show us the ropes."

"You'll pick it right up," Jim laughed. "It's not hard, and while it will be like roughing it, we'll take care of the plans and logistics. We want you to be able to love the kids and see what it's like to support these families."

As the steaks arrived, they continued talking, and Jim outlined what a deeper partnership with Chrysalis would look like. That conversation led to the Scotts making several trips overseas with Chrysalis. They joined Jim in Sudan and visited a Chrysalis team in Lebanon. As their connection with Chrysalis deepened, so did their commitment to the work. Their financial support increased as well.

CELEBRATION

"Wow!" Chad's draw dropped. "Look at that view!"

"Amazing," Fred echoed.

"We told you!" Ann, Olivia, and Elisa grinned triumphantly at their husbands. "We told you it would be worth it!"

"It is amazing!" Chad grinned, too. "But worth it? I'll have to think about it."

Olivia punched his shoulder. Worth it!

He laughed, "You're right. I take it all back. The hike was worth it, the view is amazing, and we got to hang out together. It has been a great afternoon."

They gazed out over the snowcapped mountain peaks. The late afternoon sun lit the peaks in hues of gold, purple, pink, and red. The peaks marched on in an endless array, one rocky outcrop giving way to another as far as the eye could see. They watched the sun slide toward the furthest peaks to the West and the purple shades darken in the valleys between the peaks.

Ann turned to the others regretfully. "I guess we'd better head back down for dinner," she said. "I would hate to have to negotiate that path in the dark. And, of course, we don't want to miss dinner and tonight's celebration."

"Nope. You're right. We'd better get rolling." Jim turned away and moved back toward the trail down to the hotel. The others followed him as he started back down the trail. In the glow of early twilight, the aspens seemed to glow, and the darker greens of the firs contrasted vividly with the rocks and stones of the path. The fading warmth of the sun, the fresh scent of pine, and the dying breeze whispering through the trees lent a mystical quality to the evening. A quiet sense of well-being filled them as they wound their way back down toward the hotel. Those trips deeply impacted Fred and Elisa, Jim mused, as he wound his way back down the trail at the head of the group.

DONORS TO CHAMPIONS: CHAMPION

The Scotts had seen firsthand what their donations of funds, time, and engagement had done for the children and families in Sudan and Lebanon. Elisa seemed to have found her niche. She was writing regularly to a group of single mothers in one of the Lebanese camps where Chrysalis was heavily engaged, and she remained in regular contact with several orphaned children she had met in Sudan. In fact, she was planning on helping one of the older girls visit the United States in the next couple of months.

As their engagement with Chrysalis deepened, their commitment to the organization became even more evident. Over the past several years, they had become more active advocates for Chrysalis's mission. It was amazing, Jim thought, the way the two of them had become such raving fans of the organization. Both Fred and Elisa bubbled over with excitement whenever they got the chance to talk about Chrysalis. They had introduced several friends to Chrysalis, and they were always looking for ways to connect Chrysalis with additional friends and other organizations.

CELEBRATION

Almost without realizing it, Jim found himself coming to the bottom of the path. The lights from the hotel sparkled brightly in the dying light and offered an invitation to the warmth within. The others were just behind him as they reached the paved trail that led through the meadow in front of the hotel.

They really were Chrysalis champions, Jim thought as he looked back at Fred and Elisa. They loved and trusted Chrysalis, and now they were as much a part of the organization as he was.

Suddenly, Jim realized that everyone was looking at him and laughing. He looked at Ann, "What's so funny?"

Ann chuckled, "Olivia, Elisa, and I were just noting that you certainly didn't have any trouble coming back down the trail! Obviously, you were more concerned about getting back for a good meal than seeing the view. You didn't say a word on the way down. You just said, 'Follow me,' and took off."

Jim blushed. "I'm sorry, guys. I guess I got lost in my thoughts and didn't realize I was racing back down the trail."

"It's okay, Jim. We know how it is when you start thinking about food, you just can't stop!" Chad teased.

"Yeah," Ann chimed in, "I mean, you know what they say about turning the horse toward the barn."

"I wasn't thinking about food," Jim protested, "at least not the whole time."

"Right," Olivia said, straight-faced, "only about 99 percent of the time."

Elisa came to Jim's rescue. "You can hardly blame him," she said, laughing. "The food is fantastic, and we did drag him up and down the mountain!"

"All right, all right." Jim began herding everyone toward the doors of the hotel. "We have to get moving. As you all so kindly noted, I want to eat, and I wouldn't mind a shower before dinner. So, if you're done harassing me, perhaps we could head in that direction." Still joking and laughing, they all hurried into the hotel and headed for their various rooms.

CELEBRATION

"Wow! You look beautiful."

"Thanks, Hon. Can you help me with this necklace?" Ann looked critically at her hair in the mirror. "I can't seem to get these curls right."

"Your hair looks great to me," Jim grunted as he fumbled with the clasp on the necklace.

"Oh, you always say that!"

Ann fumed as she twisted another strand of hair. "You just want to get to dinner!"

"Well," Jim laughed, "that's true, but you really do look great." In her black dress and diamond earrings, Ann did look striking. Together they headed out the door and down to dinner.

The rear terrace on the back of the hotel was a stunning affair. Large stone pavers covered the ground, and beautiful stone balustrades ran the entire length of the terrace. The beautiful gas lamps in the corners were set off by inset terrace lighting, as well as beautiful miniature lamps on the tables. The light danced, flickering off the glasses and the silver table settings. The round tables were covered in white tablecloths with beautiful floral arrangements placed in the center.

A spectacular buffet had been set up on one side of the terrace so as not to block the view of the mountains in the background. The buffet was magnificent. A trio of salads was followed by a wonderful selection of appetizers including fresh shrimp, which looked amazing, Ann thought. Her mouth watered when she saw the oysters.

As Jim went to find their table, she wandered along the buffet. Green beans, mixed vegetable grill, and sweet potato soufflé! One dish gave way to another, each looking better than the last. Ann wondered how in the world she could try them all.

Jim rejoined her just as she reached the carving table.

"Just in time for your favorite part, I see," she teased as he admired the prime rib.

"Yep. You can keep all that froufrou food, and I'll do some real damage down at this end. Just look at that prime rib. And it looks like they have some buffalo ribs as well."

"That should keep you happy," Ann laughed. "Where are we sitting?"

"We're at that table in the front, close to that little dais.

Koen and Cheryl are already there. Do you see them?"

"Okay, then. I'm going to head over and drop my purse," Ann said.

"Sounds great. I'm just going to say hi to a few folks as they come in. I'll join you in a minute." Jim hurried off to greet the guests emerging from the hotel onto the terrace.

"Over here!" Cheryl Ridder saw Ann and waved. She gave Ann a quick hug as she walked up. Cheryl was a good counterpoint to Koen, Ann thought, petite with brown hair, glasses, and a soft motherly air about her; she softened some of her husband's harder edges.

"Ann!" Koen boomed. "I'm so glad you're here!

Where's that husband of yours gotten off to?"

"He's off greeting guests." Ann hugged Koen before settling into her chair.

"Always working, that's Jim," Koen said. "This place wouldn't be the same without him."

"Jim's a real saint," Cheryl agreed. "How have you been, Ann? Are you enjoying the hotel?"

"The entire weekend has been wonderful!" Ann's eyes sparkled. "The hotel's beautiful. We had a wonderful hike with some long-time ministry partners, and, of course, I always enjoy hearing about all Chrysalis is doing around the world. The magnitude of this organization's impact never ceases to amaze me. Of course, we are all wondering what Koen's special announcement is going to be."

"What's that?" Koen caught the tail end of Ann's comments, and he grinned mysteriously. "Not long now," he chuckled. "But, like everyone else, you'll just have to wait!"

"He's been so mysterious about all of this," Cheryl complained, looking over at her husband in disgust. "He won't even let me in on his secret!"

"Wouldn't be much of a secret if I started letting everyone in on it, now, would it?" Koen smirked.

"I'm not 'everyone.' I'm your new wife!" Cheryl shot back.

"Men," she turned back to Ann. "What can you do with them? I guess we just love them and let them have their little secrets."

Ann laughed and rolled her eyes at Cheryl.

"Oh, look. There's Tom and Mandi." Cheryl waved excitedly.

As the pair strolled up, Tom eyed Ann and winked. "You look younger every time I see you," he said.

"What a sweet talker," Ann blushed. "How did you ever end up in accounting, Tom?"

"He is smooth and crafty," Mandi said, "but he's mostly honest."

"The abuse," Tom moaned. "Try to pay a lady a compliment, and see what happens." Tom and Koen shook hands as Mandi joined Ann and Cheryl at the table.

"I'm sure Jim's off chatting," Tom said, "so I guess we're just missing Kristin and Matt.

"I'm sure they'll be along shortly," Koen said, taking the chair next to his wife, Cheryl. "Sit down and join us, Tom. We'll get everything kicked off in a few minutes."

A few minutes later, Jim walked up with Kristin and Matt in tow. "I found these two strays sneaking tidbits from the dessert table," he grinned. Matt was as thin as a rail and looked like he could use more than a few good desserts.

Tom and Koen laughed, and Matt grinned. "Just trying to keep up with you, old boy." Matt's British accent made them all laugh.

"That's impossible, Matt. My husband eats more than you and Tom put together," said Ann.

"I don't know where he puts it," Koen grumbled. "The man's as thin as the day I met him."

"Oh, it's the running, I'm sure," Cheryl smiled at Jim.

"I run too," Koen protested.

"Well, honey," Cheryl smiled sweetly up at him, "maybe you're just not putting in enough miles." Everyone joined in the laughter as they settled into their seats. A few minutes later, the emcee directed their table to the buffet, and they all headed off to get dinner.

The next hour passed in a happy blur as they sampled the delicious items arrayed on the buffet and chatted about children and grandchildren as well as all Chrysalis had accomplished throughout the year.

Jim sighed contentedly, leaning back in his chair, nursing a cup of coffee, and eyeing the last small bit of French silk pie on his plate. "Maybe I should have another piece of pie," he said.

"I'm amazed you can make it back to the buffet," Koen teased, "you must have had at least four slices of that prime rib."

Jim grinned. "I worked hard this afternoon, Koen. My wife hauled me up and down a mountain. I need to make up for all the calories I burned." Ann rolled her eyes at him.

"Then you'd better get that piece of pie now, Jim. The program's about to begin, and I want to be sure you're sitting right here when I finally share my secret." Koen's eyes gleamed in the light from the table.

"Too late," Ann whispered. While Koen and Jim were talking, the emcee moved back up onto the dais. The crowd gradually quieted, and he launched into the agenda for the evening.

"Tonight," he began, "we have something special planned. Koen Ridder is going to give us a brief update on some key ministry objectives, and then I understand he has a special announcement to share. Following Koen's announcement, we'll move back to the ballroom for a special showing of the new Chrysalis impact video."

Koen took the dais and looked out over the crowd. The evening mountain air swept over the crowd as the warm lights flickered across a sea of expectant faces. Over the next several minutes, Koen held his listeners entranced as he shared about the tremendous impact that Chrysalis was making around the world. In the midst of conflict and confusion, Chrysalis sowed the light of Christ on a broken world. Feeding children, caring for families, bringing hope to those who had lost hope. Koen spoke of their efforts to provide safe, sanitary lodging in refugee camps in the Sudan and medical care in Lebanon. He spoke of the impact of initiatives around the conflict in Haiti. "All around the world, wherever there is significant conflict, Chrysalis is there, shining hope and offering support," Koen finished.

He paused and let the silence build for a few moments. "And now," he said, and he smiled. The audience on the edge of their seats, he began, "Over the last ten years, we have laid out a plan for funding this organization's efforts around the world. All of you have partnered with us in the effort. It has not always been easy, but thanks to your willingness to trust our team, we have experienced significant growth over the last decade. I am thrilled to announce tonight that we have met our goal of establishing a 50-million-dollar endowment to offset the administrative cost of our efforts. We have also received an additional immediate gift of 30 million dollars from an estate. Half of this gift was designated by the donor to build our endowment, allowing us to devote a larger percentage of every future gift to our ongoing projects around the world."

The terrace rang with applause at this announcement.

Koen waited for the clapping to die down. "This phenomenal achievement is only possible because of your generosity. Each of you has played a part in rebuilding this organization and allowing us to expand our impact around the world. Together, you have testified to the worthiness of this organization and its mission. And together we will continue to offer a beacon of hope to those who have been displaced by armed conflict around the globe!"

As the applause died away, Jim looked up into the stars shining in a clear night sky. They had done it! Together, he, Koen, and the Chrysalis team had embarked on a journey along the worthiness continuum. They transformed a dying organization into a well-funded beacon of hope to a lost world.

PART TWO

THE MODEL

INTRODUCTION

I want you to close your eyes. Take a moment to create an image of what the fulfillment of your organization's mission and vision will look like. What would it look like if you were fully funded and could pursue that vision without financial restraint? How could that impact the lives of the people you serve and the communities you touch? This is the type of vision I want you to invite your donors to invest in. But vision alone isn't enough to earn your donor's trust.

Both you and your organization need to be worthy of the funds a donor invests. The Bible is clear that we need to be faithful with worldly wealth. Luke 16:11 says that if you have not been faithful with worldly wealth, then who will entrust you with true riches? This verse from scripture highlights the fact that our faithfulness with the funds entrusted to us is really what drives future organizational vision achievement. But how do you prove your personal worthiness and the worthiness of your organization?

In this book, you will learn to build a trusting relationship with donors, and you will develop the skills you need to communicate your ability to steward a large gift. You will also demonstrate your organization's worthiness of greater gifts through a proven method that will help you earn the trust of your donors, put the necessary policies and procedures in place, and develop a plan that will help you build a relationship with key donors you want to become champions for your organization. Let's be honest. Asking people to give is hard, and it can be uncomfortable if you don't have a clear plan. I wrote this book because I want to equip you and your team so that you are ready and you have a plan when the opportunity arises.

I also wrote this book because I care about our donors. Wealth can be isolating, and even when you have the desire to be generous, it's hard to know where to give. It's important that we come alongside those with resources so they see the opportunity their wealth gives them to invest in something lasting and worthy of their sacrifice. Ultimately, that's your calling, and that is what this book will equip you to do.

CHAPTER 1

WORTHINESS

Worthiness. In our day and time, we don't talk a lot about worthiness because we don't want anyone to feel unworthy. And I think we would all agree that every human is fundamentally worthy because we are made in God's image. Koen and Jim introduced us to 'worthiness' in the Fable. Clearly, in the case of your charity, like in the case of Chrysalis, I am talking about more than intrinsic value. I am talking about worthiness as it is determined by others, particularly the donors of your organization.

A worthy organization exhibits faithfulness, knowledge, dependability, perseverance, and meticulous stewardship. These qualities allow donors to connect to your organization in a deeper way. Donors long to connect to something greater than themselves, and by offering a worthy pursuit, you can draw them into a meaningful partnership.

You want donors to believe in your organizational vision and mission, to understand your organization is faithful, dependable, and will meticulously steward their gifts. This is organizational worthiness.

As you partner with donors, you want to persevere as a trusted advisor and exhibit skills that exceed a donor's expectations and merit their confidence as they consider the stewardship of their resources. This is individual worthiness.

The Fable talks a lot about worthiness, both organizational and individual worthiness, because I believe worthiness encompasses the key characteristics donors utilize to determine where to give their time, talent, and treasure. Worthiness is critical because it ties directly to donor trust. A donor might make a gift to your organization, but no donor will make a significant investment in an organization unless they believe the organization and its leadership are truly worthy of that investment.

I believe many organizations are worthy of investment, but they don't know how to communicate that worthiness. Other organizations are struggling. They have a great mission, but many elements of worthiness prove to be elusive. They may struggle to connect their mission to their vision. They may have some dedicated volunteers and a few committed donors, but they haven't been able to grow their base of supporters. They need real help.

Wherever you are on the continuum of worthiness, this book can help you define and communicate your worthiness to donors.

Worthiness begins with the vision and mission of your organization, but it encompasses so much more.

Worthiness is also linked to the knowledge, passion, and stewardship philosophy of your fundraising team.

Worthiness is communicated through an intentional relationship with your donors that reveals why a donor should trust you with a significant gift of time, talent, or treasure.

And finally, worthiness is about confidence, the confidence you elicit from your donors because you are confident in your own processes and skills. Like Koen, Jim, and April, you want to be able to answer your donors' questions, but beyond that, you want to be confident that you are equipped to shepherd your donors' hearts as well as manage their gifts.

Organizational worthiness leads to donor trust.

Demonstrating organizational worthiness involves casting vision, executing missions, and building a relationship with donors. This process doesn't happen overnight. It is an ongoing process that never truly ends for any organization funded by donations.

If you are a nonprofit, a transformational gift isn't the answer to all your problems. In fact, large gifts can be very complicated to receive. But a transformational gift can be a game-changer as far as fulfilling your vision and mission.

I wrote this book and the Fable about Chrysalis to help you enhance your organization's worthiness so that you are prepared, you have a plan, and your organization is ready to secure and manage those big transformational gifts. I have seen firsthand that when vision is heard and funds are committed, lives can be changed!

CHAPTER 2

ORGANIZATIONAL WORTHINESS

When we demonstrate worthiness, we develop the trust of our donors. So, how do we go about proving worthiness at the organizational level? As Koen highlighted in the Fable, we begin with vision.

Vision connects people with something larger than themselves and taps into the deep need we all possess to know that our participation and contribution matter. When you give money, even a small amount, you want to know it is going to do something important, something meaningful, and that your sacrifice makes a difference. When you communicate your organization's vision, you want to connect people with what you are trying to accomplish so they feel like their generosity is an essential part of fulfilling the vision. You can't do it without them!

Perhaps you're trying to help children around the world. Maybe you're trying to enhance faith-based education, or maybe you're trying to provide funding for at-risk people in different places around the world. All of these are great visions that seek to make a significant impact, transform lives, and contribute to the flourishing of communities.

You want to create alignment between your organization's vision and the donor's vision by connecting their passion to what you are seeking to accomplish.

The mission is what accomplishes the vision. How does the mission of your organization fulfill its vision? You must be able to articulate the mission clearly and straightforwardly that connects the dots between the donor's gift and what your organization is trying to accomplish.

If your vision is helping children around the world, do you invite donors to send a shoe box each year to needy children, or do you ask them to be a monthly sponsor? If you want to enhance faith-based education, what does that look like? Does their gift develop curriculum, train teachers, or provide scholarships? It's not enough to have a vision that promises impact. You must have a plan that connects donors with the mission, the 'how' that fulfills the vision.

Everyone on your team and even in your organization needs to be able to communicate the vision and mission of your organization clearly and concisely. As you think about these things, it's important to know what makes your organization unique. How do your vision and mission differ from those of other organizations, and especially from other similar organizations? This is a question your whole team needs to be able to answer, because if a donor is passionate about the things you are doing, they will most likely know about other organizations doing similar things. You need to be able to tell potential donors why they should invest in your organization's vision and mission specifically.

Koen introduced us to Chrysalis's vision, but let me share a real-life example with you. I was recently at an event for an aviation ministry that uses airplanes to reach isolated people with the Gospel, and, as I looked around, I realized how many people there were pilots, people who had a passion for flying. This makes sense because their passion for flying aligns with the organization's key pillars of planes, people, and impact. So, at this event, the aviation ministry knew and shared their vision and mission in a way that aligned with the donors' passions for flying. They invited donors to invest in flying as a way to reach isolated people with the Gospel. The event was very successful and raised a significant amount of money for the ministry.

As you can see from this example, connecting a donor's passion to the mission and vision of your organization is a powerful way to build connections. Ultimately, it is that connection with a donor that leads to a significant gift. In the Fable, we were introduced to multiple donors who connected with Chrysalis's vision *to offer hope to those displaced by armed conflict around the globe.*

You want major donors to trust your organization.

Having a clearly stated vision and mission that everyone on your donor development team knows provides the foundation for trust. Now, let's get into the finer details of organizational worthiness.

In the story, Tom and Jim worked with Koen to improve the internal governance structure at Chrysalis. Like them, you must ensure that you comply with federal and state legal guidelines that support your organization's status as a nonprofit, and you must be able to clearly and simply articulate that you're in compliance and following organizational best practices. So many large organizations have failed to meet ethical standards in managing resources. This means all organizations need to go above and beyond to prove the gifts they are given really do serve the purposes for which they were intended. Implementing best practices and subjecting your organization to third-party scrutiny is a critical component in proving your organization's worthiness and demonstrating you can handle the next level of financial gift. There are Three Keys to assessing your organization's worthiness. They are **Transparency, Prudency, and Fiduciary**.

For **transparency**, your organization's compliance with the normal legal guidelines of a 501(c)(3) nonprofit needs to be validated and communicated. You can't say you are building wells in Africa if you aren't. You can't tell donors their gift will be spent on translating the Bible if you are really spending it on something else.

When talking about transparency, what we are really talking about is assuring your donor that your financial house is in order and that you have the proper internal governance policies in place to effectively manage their gift.

The Evangelical Council for Financial Accountability, or ECFA, helps certify organizations. The ECFA assures donors that your organization is taking care of the funds entrusted to them. Transparency around the financial policies and procedures of your organization communicates that you take accountability seriously and helps build the trust of your donors.

For **prudency**, the Uniform Prudent Management of Institutional Funds Act, or UPMIFA, provides guidance and authority to charitable organizations concerning the management and investment of funds. UPMIFA also helps guide and protect the interests of income and remainder beneficiaries.

UPMIFA provides direction to organizations regarding how the funds entrusted to them are to be managed.

UPMIFA's guidance may be summarized by understanding and observing its four key principles:

1. Investment funds entrusted to your organization should be diversified.
2. Investment fiduciaries should act with care, skill, and prudence in the investment of funds entrusted to them.
3. The costs incurred in the management of funds must be reasonable.
4. Distribution rates for endowment funds should generally be indefinitely sustainable. In other words, the distribution rate should not be so high as to exhaust the funds.

Generally, UPMIFA applies to endowment funds, but several of its key principles apply more broadly to other funds entrusted to nonprofits. You should become familiar with UPMIFA guidelines to ensure your organization meets the appropriate prudency standard.

Finally, a **fiduciary** is a legal term that describes a person or organization that acts on behalf of another person or persons, putting their clients' interests ahead of their own, with a duty to preserve good faith and trust. Being a fiduciary thus requires being bound both legally and ethically to act in the beneficiary's best interests.

As a fiduciary, it's important to define the beneficiary of your organization. There are often multiple beneficiaries. The first two, the donor and the people affected by your organization's vision and mission, or clients, are easy to recognize. The third is more complicated because it could be another organization or an income beneficiary of a split-interest gift. If you set up a split-interest gift, like a charitable trust, a gift-annuity program, a pooled income fund, or even a donor advised fund, other organizations may be receiving assets from you. Or there may be an individual other than the original donor who's receiving an income stream from your organization. In cases where the funds distribute an income stream, you have a clear fiduciary duty to manage funds entrusted to you on behalf of both the income beneficiary and the ultimate charitable beneficiary.

As a fiduciary, you need to consider how you assess reasonable costs when investing funds and how you establish a reasonable distribution pattern for the funds that are entrusted to you. We will talk more about being a fiduciary when we talk about reporting.

Understanding your legal responsibility as a fiduciary impacts both your philosophies and your policies and ultimately deepens trust with your donors and constituents.

These Three Keys—transparency, prudency, and fiduciary—help donors assess your organization's worthiness. As you seek donor engagement, communication around these keys is critical to building a deeper level of trust with donors and ensuring they see you as prepared to receive a more significant gift.

CHAPTER 3

IMPLEMENTING ORGANIZATIONAL WORTHINESS THROUGH POLICIES & PROCEDURES

All organizations have policies and procedures. Even the smallest organization must have some track to run on. Many of these policies and procedures are unwritten but are nonetheless important to ensure the smooth operation of the nonprofit. We will not delve into all the systems and policies necessary for a nonprofit to function effectively in the marketplace. Instead, I will highlight key policies and procedures that I believe help move an organization along the worthiness continuum in the eyes of the donor. These policies and procedures directly impact the donor's trust.

They relate to the acceptance, management, and distribution of financial gifts.

The development team is responsible for engaging with donors, building relationships, and securing gifts for the organization. The finance department is often tasked with managing, receipting, administering, and distributing those gifts after they are received. At Chrysalis, Jim and Tom worked together to address these issues and modeled a positive relational "bridge" between the finance and development departments.

There is often a bit of a disconnect between finance and development. The finance department can be very conservative when it comes to accepting gifts, which in and of itself is not a bad thing. This can be frustrating for development when they have an opportunity with a donor that involves a more complicated gift. Instead of working together, the two departments can feel like they are working against each other. Some have even called finance the "sales prevention office."

So, how do you build a bridge between finance and development? It begins with communication and coordination. The goal is to equip each department to manage its area of responsibility while, at the same time, working with the other departments. Finance needs to know what type of gifts to expect and when, as it stewards the assets. Development articulates the organization's vision and mission, working with donors to secure gifts but not promising something they can't deliver.

Clearly defined philosophies and policies are critical elements in coordinating the efforts of these two departments. The **gift acceptance policy** defines the types of gifts your organization is willing to receive and helps provide comfort and consistency for the finance team.

Establishing exception guidelines is also important. Both teams need to know how to process gifts that might be beyond the scope of your gift acceptance policy. As development officers, we try not to say no, but if a gift does not fit within the parameters of your gift acceptance policy, you need to have a plan in place. You'll need a standard to share with the donor before you spend too much time pursuing a gift your organization can't handle.

In the story, Koen worked to get an investment committee set up. That committee worked with Tom and Jim to select a consultant, "FAC," who assisted Chrysalis in developing its investment philosophy and investment policies. Your organization's **investment philosophy** and **investment policies** define how funds are managed. Both the gift acceptance policy and investment philosophy should inform the policies and procedures developed by the finance department.

Without clear philosophies that translate into executable policies and procedures, conflict can arise between the finance and development departments. Experiencing confusion, mixed messages, or worse, the frustration of one or both departments, can destroy a donor's trust and undermine the funding you are seeking.

Donors need to know that when they give a gift, there is a plan in place to facilitate and manage it. Communication and continuity between the finance and development departments are critical to building the trust of donors and establishing organizational worthiness.

CHAPTER 4

INVESTMENT PHILOSOPHY

As part of your organization's worthiness, it is important to develop an investment philosophy. Your organizational investment philosophy determines exactly how your organization views money that's entrusted to it, particularly money that's been entrusted for investment purposes, like an endowment, a charitable trust, a gift annuity program, or other reserve or operating funds.

Having a clearly defined philosophy helps avoid confusion, aligns board members' and staff expectations, and should guide policy development. Ultimately, this philosophy answers the question:

What core beliefs about investing do we as an organization have that will affect the funds that have been entrusted to us?

In spiritual terms, you might consider this your organization's "world view" of investing. While many important components make up a comprehensive investment philosophy, the most important elements can be distilled from the following four questions:

- What do you believe about asset allocation?
- Why is diversification important?
- What do you believe about market timing?
- What do you believe about social screening and biblically responsible investing?

The answer to these questions will help you define your organization's philosophical position and ultimately act as the guiding source for your investment policy. You need to be sure your investment philosophy is well articulated and flows through to your written investment policies. Remember, philosophy drives policy.

Investment philosophy acts as both a guide and guard for your organization's investment program.

It is a **guide** because it aligns all key stakeholders with a set of guiding principles.

Its principles are a **guard,** protecting the investment program from getting into areas that could cause problems for the organization or its constituents.

For example, one of your philosophical positions is that diversification is always important for institutional funds because it provides the protection of statutory law (UPMIFA, for example). If a new board member joins your board and says he believes the organization should concentrate all its assets in just a couple of stocks, it becomes relatively easy to explain to that board member that while he may personally believe a concentrated portfolio is a better choice, that position doesn't fit with the investment philosophy the organization has adopted.

Having generally accepted philosophical investment positions also helps gain the trust of donors. This is similar to a doctrinal statement outlining what you believe spiritually. A donor may not agree with every single point, but they know where you stand, and, consequently, they know what to expect.

Let me share an example with you. I was once presenting an asset allocation study to an endowment investment committee. The organization had worked through philosophical issues and was considering adding this asset class as an acceptable investment alternative to its investment policy.

A new member of the committee, in his very first meeting, challenged the philosophical assumption that this particular asset class should even be considered, as it was, in his view, too risky! Rather, he thought the committee should focus in a completely different direction.

The chair responded very respectfully, but very firmly, and suggested the new member read all the materials pertinent to this investment. The chair continued by suggesting the new member not speak until he better understood the philosophical framework that had already been developed and was guiding this particular decision.

Finally, if he could not get on board with the philosophy, then perhaps he was on the wrong committee.

In this case, the organization had already made philosophical decisions about diversification and how to manage risk through asset allocation. That philosophical framework guided the ultimate discussion of how to implement the framework through policy. The chairman's understanding of the philosophy helped keep the meeting from being derailed and allowed the committee to make informed decisions.

Articulating your organization's investment philosophy grounds your policies and helps protect your organization.

CHAPTER 5

CONSTRUCTING AN INVESTMENT PHILOSOPHY

Let's take a closer look at what it means to understand and articulate our organization's investment philosophy:

What core beliefs about investing do we as an organization have that will affect the funds that have been entrusted to us?

As I said, in spiritual terms, this is your organization's worldview of investing. To answer this question, we need to dig more deeply into the first two key questions I mentioned:

What do you believe about asset allocation? Why is diversification important?

Now, before I begin, I need you to understand that many of the answers are connected. For instance, it is difficult to talk about asset allocation if one doesn't understand the basic benefits of diversification. Our goal in this journey is to simplify these challenging concepts. So, please know there is much more to know than we will cover in this book.

Let's start with the first question:

What do you believe about asset allocation?

At its core, asset allocation is about asset classes. An asset class may be thought of as a similar grouping of securities or investment alternatives. For example, stocks, bonds, cash, precious metals, and real estate are all examples of asset classes. The way you go about combining those asset classes can be thought of as asset allocation. Further, each asset class has its own risk and return characteristics. By combining those asset classes, you create portfolios with different risk and return parameters.

The fact that you are combining classes of securities suggests the concept of diversification is both important and present in your investment portfolio. We'll get to diversification in a moment. For now, you must understand that most organizations agree that asset allocation is important, and a portfolio comprises one or more asset classes. Think stocks, bonds, and cash, for example.

However, how you gain exposure to that asset class becomes a key philosophical question.

There are two primary methodologies for gaining asset class exposure: active and passive.

An **active strategy** seeks to pick stocks, bonds, or other securities that outperform a simple broad index comprising those securities. Simply stated, it is an implementation methodology that seeks to invest to beat the market in an active manner.

A **passive strategy** accepts the market, or index, returns in a given area at a lower cost point. As stated, it doesn't try to beat the market. A passive strategy simply tries to replicate the corresponding index of securities. For example, the S&P 500 is an index of large U.S. companies. Investors can either pick specific companies to try to beat the market or simply replicate the S&P 500, minus the cost of replication. Either way, you have exposure to the large US stocks as an asset class, but the results could be significantly different.

The philosophical argument here centers on efficiency.

If the market is extremely efficient, then no strategy can outperform because all information is reflected in current pricing. If that is the case, then you should simply utilize a low-cost strategy and passively replicate the market.

However, many investors believe that picking securities involves skill and that perhaps markets are not fully efficient. They believe investors can beat the market either by lowering risk, enhancing return, or sometimes utilizing a combination of the two. This is a common and well-known debate, and most major donors are aware of it. They will want to know where your organization stands on this issue so they can manage expectations regarding an endowment they hold with your organization or perhaps a charitable trust your organization is managing on their behalf.

The second question is:

Why is diversification important?

As we have noted, UPMIFA assumes diversification is equivalent to prudence. There is a balance, or trade-off, between risk and return, which is why it is so important to diversify. In a diversified portfolio, the loss of any single security will not be detrimental to the long-term performance of the portfolio. Generally speaking, you need to diversify. Again, this concept is sometimes problematic for board members or donors who have made a lot of money in a single stock or large piece of real estate.

However, when they understand the fiduciary nature of your organization and its responsibility of stewardship to multiple beneficiaries, they can better accept this philosophical position.

What do you believe about market timing?

This question is often also related to asset allocation and diversification, but at its core, it surrounds the concept of foresight. Market timing really relates to trying to time a significant change in the market. It can be absolute. For example, if you believe the market is going down, you might simply sell everything and go to cash. However, if you are wrong, the outcome could be catastrophic. Even if you get out of the market before a major decline, you must also know when to get back into the market. This sort of strategy is rarely effective in the long term. Eventually, a mistake is likely. In contrast, a strategic long-term asset allocation strategy employs a more static approach relying on diversification and the corresponding correlation benefits brought about by that diversification to lower volatility and protect the portfolio. Often, in institutional circles, it is understood that a strategic approach to asset allocation with, perhaps, a minor amount of tactical overlay, fits better with UPMIFA and a fiduciary mandate. Regardless, the important element is that your organization clearly delineates the position it is taking.

And finally, let's look at this question:

What do you believe about social screening and values-based investing?

Because awareness of socially responsible investing has grown in recent years, we'll talk about this issue later. Initially, from a philosophical standpoint, you must understand how your organization views this issue. Social screening, or values-based investing, focuses beyond the immediate economics of the investment and looks deeper to understand how the investment impacts other components that are important to the investor or to society at large.

For example, some values-based concerns might include the environment, social constructs like avoiding slave labor, and similar issues. For many faith-based organizations, this may begin with screening out objectionable practices and then expand to reflect positive values by investing in companies that encourage human flourishing or bring redemption to a community.

The key here is that, philosophically, your organization must maintain a clear position governing how they are responding to these issues in its investment portfolios.

Again, donors do not always have to fully agree, but trust is built through clarity and transparency. The fact that your organization has carefully considered the issue and developed a well-considered philosophical position will inspire the donor's trust. As an ambassador of your organization, you need to be able to communicate these important philosophical positions to your donors to help establish trust and credibility.

CHAPTER 6

INVESTMENT PHILOSOPHY SOCIAL SCREENING

An important element of organizational worthiness is the development of an investment philosophy. We have already noted that philosophy must address socially responsible investing or biblically responsible investing. Values alignment is a complex and ever-changing component of the investment world, and I want to take a more comprehensive look at some key terms and strategies that should be addressed through your organization's philosophy.

So, for example, biblically responsible investing may screen out "sin stocks" like alcohol, tobacco, gambling, abortions, pornography, or the sex industry, and, even in some cases, defense. This is a negative screen that might be associated with traditional Christian values.

On the other hand, we may have positive screens in place. This means simply investing in companies that promote human flourishing, encourage generous practices, or value employees and communities, thus reflecting biblical values.

As you consider social screening and biblically responsible investing, there are three basic acronyms you need to know:

Environmental, Social, and Governance, or ESG, is a set of standards and guidelines that help you evaluate an investment according to its environmental impact, social responsibility, and organizational governance.

Environmental concerns might include things like green energy or pollution policies, while a socially responsible investment might consider working conditions, fair compensation, and treatment of labor. Governance considerations look at a company's oversight and how it is governed. For example, a company may be managed by a board and investors. Governance also dictates proxy considerations and company transparency.

Socially Responsible Investing, or SRI, is investing that reflects the investor's values or the values of the nonprofit entity through their investment methodology. SRI involves screening-in an investment for positive policies, like green energy, and screening-out investments for negative practices, like a company with a history of pollution.

Finally, BRI stands for Biblically Responsible Investing. This means you are choosing investments that reflect the biblical values of your organization.

It's essential for your organization to define its position related to BRI, SRI, and ESG. This position must be articulated in the form of policy because, ultimately, that policy will contribute to your worthiness as an organization. Your donors want to know where you and your organization stand on each of these screening issues. It's okay if the donor doesn't directly agree with your position. Even when you disagree, donors appreciate the fact that you have taken the time to articulate a position and support it. The most important thing in demonstrating worthiness is to have a well-articulated position on how you're going to address social and faith-based values in your investment screening process.

CHAPTER 7

INVESTMENT POLICY

Philosophy drives what we do. Policy is the roadmap that articulates how you implement your philosophy. Now that we have clarified investment philosophy, the next step is explaining investment policy.

An investment policy is a written statement that defines how a particular portfolio will be invested. You want to summarize how the funds will be invested, what you want to achieve through the investment program, and document your implementation plan. The policy should document key considerations, like goals, constraints, and risk tolerance. It should also reflect the outcome of your organization's portfolio design process.

Begin your investment policy statement by outlining the facts and circumstances surrounding a particular pool of assets. Summarize what you want to accomplish with this particular pool of assets. Summarize key objectives, designate appropriate risk tolerance for the pool, and summarize any constraints that may act as limiting factors in your investment program for this particular pool.

For example, an endowment's objective may be long-term growth to support the organization's mission. The endowment's time horizon is indefinite, and, under normal circumstances, its risk tolerance would be relatively high. However, the endowment is constrained by UPMIFA and the need to make regular distributions back to the organization. The endowment could also be constrained by social screening criteria.

Ultimately, the policy framework outlines the return objective and distribution rate for the endowment and provides clarity around the organization's willingness and ability to take risks to meet those objectives. The policy provides an overview of the type of investment plan the organization intends to utilize to meet these objectives, and it concludes with an asset allocation and implementation plan that can be followed by the organization's investment consultant. In many cases, the organization's investment consultant will assist with the development of the investment policy.

In the story, Doug spent a significant amount of time with Liam and Warren developing investment policies for Chrysalis. Your investment policies tell the investment consultant exactly how to invest money.

CHAPTER 8

REPORTING

Building donor trust by demonstrating organizational worthiness requires an effective reporting structure that communicates how you are managing the funds entrusted to your organization. Reporting to donors connects the dots so they get to see the outcomes of their investment and verify that your organization is holding itself accountable. Customized reporting is essential if you hope to ask donors for a major gift.

There are a few things to consider as you develop a reporting strategy.

- **Align with your audience.** Consider your audience when creating your content. Reporting to an internal management committee or a committee of the board is different from reporting results back to a donor. Be sure you communicate clearly, concisely, and transparently.
- **Focus on results.** Activity may be important, but you need to clearly communicate results related to your donor's gift.

For an outright gift, results may simply be the impact of your mission. For a complex split-interest gift, results may include distributions, portfolio performance, and grants made. When communicating results, you always want to provide context, which is demonstrated through the performance of appropriate benchmarks.

- **Communicate consistently**. Constituents, donors, and, when appropriate, income beneficiaries should know when to expect a report. Develop a reporting schedule and stick to it.

Connecting policy to structure means ensuring we report on any gift we receive. Reporting is a key responsibility of a fiduciary.

Earlier, we talked about your legal responsibilities as a fiduciary in managing the funds entrusted to you on behalf of a beneficiary. One of the key components of managing and administering these funds is reporting. You must communicate with the beneficiary the facts needed to protect their interest. It's important that, as an organization, you recognize that you are a fiduciary in multiple senses of the word. You have a fiduciary responsibility to your donors to complete your mission and seek to fulfill your vision. If you hold and invest funds on behalf of your donor in a trust or donor advised fund, for example, you have a fiduciary responsibility related to the funds entrusted to you. Further in many split-interest gift scenarios, you may be serving as a fiduciary for income beneficiaries and other ministries.

It's important to analyze and conform to federal and state fiduciary law, federal securities law, the ethical standards of professional associations, and changing investment and management techniques. Your reports should appropriately indicate relevant cost information and properly communicate results. The proper communication of results is essential, and that may look different for different pools of assets.

Most often, reports are designed by the finance department or an outside vendor. You need to build and design effective reporting to show the donor you are doing a good job managing the funds and that you're acting as a proper fiduciary.

Reporting is a critical part of organizational worthiness. In one situation, a donor set up a trust with a charity. In 20 years, the donor never received a report on the trust! Ultimately, the donor's trust was so eroded by the lack of communication that it resulted in the trustee being terminated. Don't let this happen to you.

As a representative of your organization, you need to be able to communicate the reports to your donors, which means you need to understand what they say and how they apply to your donors' specific situation. The reports also help a donor see that what you said their gift would do is actually being realized.

Knowing and understanding the reporting structure of your organization is an important tool in maintaining your donors' trust, proving your personal worthiness, and supporting your organization's worthiness.

CHAPTER 9

GOVERNANCE

As we wrap up the idea of organizational worthiness, let's discuss internal and external governance. Your organization must follow both legal and ethical guidelines as they pertain to internal governance as well as external governance. Policy, procedure, and structure are essential in building trust with donors as they consider a larger gift.

Like Chrysalis, every organization must set up its own internal governance structure, and the formulation of many internal governance procedures is beyond the scope of this book. Internal governance procedures are a key component of organizational worthiness, and development officers need to understand the points at which internal governance overlaps with elements of external governance that connect directly with donors and constituents. I want to clarify a few points of overlap.

First, we need to recognize that our organization's gift acceptance policy is a critical component of internal governance. This policy is developed internally, usually between the development department and the finance department. The gift acceptance policy directly impacts the donor when a gift is under consideration and is a critical component in building both internal and external trust.

Second, our investment policies are developed to provide internal guidance to the finance department and various oversight committees regarding how funds should be invested. For the development officer, the policy also becomes a form of external governance, providing clarity to the donor regarding how their gift will be managed. Remember, the investment policy ultimately protects the donor, the charity, and any other beneficiaries.

Finally, investment philosophy and various fiduciary elements we have discussed, such as ECFA membership, provide guidance for the internal governance structure. These are also critical elements of our external governance program and directly affect our donor interactions as we seek to build trust.

Development officers, management, and board members must be familiar with how their organization's internal and external governance procedures work together to help protect donors and inspire trust. Ensuring your organization has these policies and procedures in place will help build your confidence in your organization's worthiness and allow you to communicate with confidence to your donors, ultimately inspiring them to entrust more significant gifts to your organization.

CHAPTER 10

PERSONAL WORTHINESS

So far, I have primarily focused on organizational worthiness. Organizational worthiness is important, but the reality is that people don't give transformational gifts to organizations, or even in support of a common vision. As we saw in the Fable, people only give those kinds of gifts to people they trust. When Jim demonstrated personal worthiness, he was able to develop the trust of his donors. So, how do you prove your personal worthiness?

Later, I will talk in depth about developing a relationship with donors. Before I talk about our horizontal relationships with donors, I want to start by asking, "Why do you do what you do?"

Understanding the why beneath your own personal philosophy of stewardship is the foundation of personal worthiness. What do you believe, and how does your faith affect your understanding of generosity? How you utilize your time, talent, and treasure impacts both your understanding of stewardship and your engagement with the donor. God is writing a larger story, and He invites us to step out of our smaller stories to be a part of His larger story. Part of your job is connecting donors with this larger story, but you must first connect yourself.

We have all been given gifts from God to steward, but before you can tell someone else the best way to steward the gifts they have been given for God's glory and the advancement of His Kingdom, you must know yourself.

Your personal stewardship philosophy involves answering the very questions you are asking donors to answer, because giving is spiritual before it is mechanical.

- What has God given me to give away?
- Where do I want to go with my time, treasure, and talent?
- How much is enough to give?
- Where and how do my investments achieve the most impact?
- When it comes to giving generously, how much consideration do I give my family?
- Can I use my giving to impact the faith of my children?
- How does my giving reflect my faith?
- How can my giving grow my faith?
- How does the organization's vision link to my own personal vision for giving?

Once you have answered these questions and established your own personal philosophy of stewardship, you are ready to build a relationship with your donors and ask them these same kinds of questions so you can begin to understand each donor's philosophy and vision.

CHAPTER 11

SPIRITUAL BEFORE MECHANICAL

In the Fable, Jim notes: "Your personal stewardship philosophy involves answering the very questions you are asking donors to answer, because giving is spiritual before it is mechanical." This means that ultimately, fundraising is spiritual too. Engaging with donors is as much about their spiritual stewardship responsibility as it is about their financial position or unique tax situation.

"God sees our faith and finances as inseparable."

—The Treasure Principle *by Randy Alcorn*

You might have to connect donors to this truth by asking them the same questions you wrestled with as you developed your own philosophy of stewardship.

These questions get to the deeper whys related to your donors' giving, and let's be honest, they aren't easy questions to answer. As you ask these really hard questions, you can connect donors to God's larger story and how their own story fits into what God is doing.

Unlike secular entities, we have a unique opportunity to engage our donors inside a spiritual paradigm and help them see that everything they own belongs to God.

Individuals are His stewards, and he has created good works from before the foundation of the world that they may walk in them. Faith is often stepping outside conventional wisdom. Discerning how God is asking us to walk in faith requires that we connect with God first.

This discipleship of stewardship requires a relationship built on trust. Asking donors to prayerfully think through these questions and engage with you over their answers can feel very vulnerable.

Building this kind of relationship requires two things, which, if they are not present, can compromise all your efforts: continuity and care.

Continuity can be hard when there is a large turnover of representatives in the donor development department of your organization. Jim and Koen had the benefit of working together for many years and building the trust of Chrysalis's donors together. The reality is, donors need to know and be known, so they need to talk to the same person, someone who can help them with the spiritual aspect of giving.

Continuity leads into **Care.** An occasional conversation via Zoom might be fine, but more often than not, donors need to see you face-to-face. They need to look you in the eye as you talk about these topics. Like Jim, you are going to need to meet regularly with your donors.

CHAPTER 12

SELLING IN A NOT-FOR-PROFIT CONTEXT

We've talked about organizational worthiness and personal worthiness. Now I want to talk with you about what it looks like to sell in a not-for-profit context. Selling describes the "how to" of building an intentional relationship with donors.

In the Fable, I describe multiple donor engagement scenarios to help illustrate how to build a relationship with your donor. I'll review a few key points from one of Jim's engagements with Fred and Elisa to help clarify the key points in relationship building.

Jim sat down across the table from Fred. After their first round of golf, Jim stayed in touch. Fred and Elisa made a few additional small cash gifts to Chrysalis. Jim asked Fred to grab coffee so he could thank him for the most recent gift.

"So, Fred, how's Elisa doing?"

"Oh, she's fine. We're all doing fine, Jim." Fred seemed distracted and distant.

"Tell me more about your giving journey, what you're interested in, what seems exciting about Chrysalis."

Fred was quiet for a moment. "Elisa is very passionate about children," he finally said. "We haven't been able to have kids, and Elisa has always wanted children. When she saw those pictures of refugee kids, hurt by the war, losing their homes, stranded in another country, it just tore at her heart strings. She really wants to help, and I guess," he looked at the table, "I just want to do whatever I can to support her in this."

Stunned by Fred's vulnerability, Jim didn't know how to respond. They sat comfortably in silence for a few moments until Fred straightened up, clearing his throat.

"Gosh, Jim. I don't know what came over me. We hardly even know each other, and here I am unveiling my soul!"

Jim immediately recognized the mute appeal in Fred's words. He had experienced this before. Giving money was often connected to something deeper. Jim didn't rush to fill the silence, but he reached across the table and put his hand on the younger man's shoulder and looked him in the eye, seeking to convey care.

Finally, he said, "First, I am so honored that you were willing to share with me. I know what it's like to long for something deeply, and I am deeply moved by your love for your wife." Jim took a deep breath. "I know that we don't know each other well, but I want you to know that I am here because I care—even if you beat me at golf."

They spent the next hour talking about Chrysalis's mission and work to provide shelter, food, and hope to families torn apart by war. By the end of the conversation, it was evident Fred was intrigued. "Jim, Elisa, and I would like to get more involved. You mentioned this new initiative to impact an additional 2,000 refugees in Sudan. How much are you trying to raise to get this done?"

"Well, our short-term goal is a million dollars," Jim said. "We'll need more than that to continue supporting this particular refugee camp, but that will help the camp support the latest influx of refugees."

"Let me talk to Elisa." Fred finished his coffee and stood up. "I've got to head back to the office. Thanks for taking the time to get together."

As Jim continued to ask questions and engage with Fred, he was looking beyond what Fred told him, to identify his concerns and look for alignment opportunities.

He listened for possible concerns or challenges for which he might be able to pose a solution. Jim was also looking to identify Fred and Elisa's passions. Their conversation revealed Fred and Elisa's passion for children, a passion that aligned with the vision and mission of Chrysalis!

As Fred's concerns and passions were revealed, Jim took the opportunity to not only offer a potential solution but also to seek to align his passion with the mission of Chrysalis. Jim was seeking to build an intentional relationship with Fred and Elisa, not just to get another friend on social media but because he wanted to establish himself as someone who could come alongside Fred and Elisa as they steward their resources.

The Fable illustrates both selling in a not-for-profit context and intentional relationship building. I want you to see how Jim was able to identify opportunities where his donor's passion aligns with Chrysalis, and where he can provide expertise in the management of his donor's resources that he might not even know he needs. The linkage between passion, creative gifting solutions, and relational connection is what leads a donor to make a transformational gift.

Selling in a nonprofit environment is a delicate balance between the relationship side of donor development and intentionally asking donors for money. You need to do both to be effective.

The four elements required in building an intentional relationship with donors are:

1. Relate
2. Explore
3. Find
4. Fix

I will delve deeper into each of these as you learn to sell in a not-for-profit context, but it's important to understand the cyclical nature of these elements. You might touch on each of the elements in most of your conversations with a donor, and you will revisit each one as you seek to build that intentional relationship with them and ultimately ask them to commit to a gift.

CHAPTER 13

RELATE

The first step in building an intentional relationship with donors is relating.

Relating is all about developing a connection with the other person, learning to see them, and really knowing them. Donor development is about relationships. Invite your donor to coffee, lunch, or dinner and get to know them.

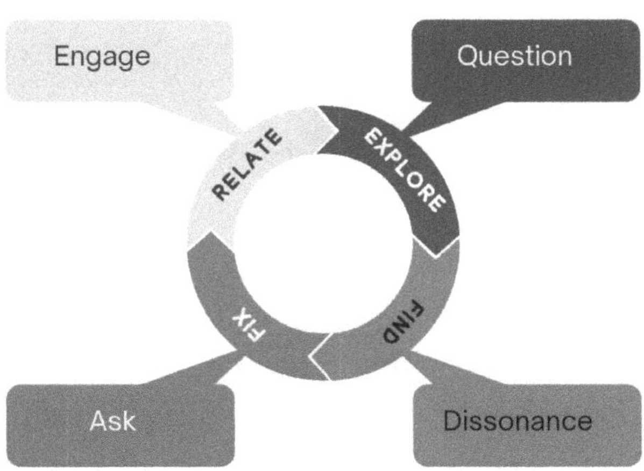

When you meet:

- **Be fully present**. Your task is the person in front of you. Nothing else is as important or should compete for your attention. Put away your phone and any other distractions and give the donor the gift of your full attention.
- **Actively listen.** We will discuss the basics of asking good questions throughout the remainder of the book, but even before you ask good questions, you need to learn to listen well. That means making eye contact, thinking about what the person is saying rather than what you will say next, and really seeking to understand, not just what is said but also what is not said. Remember, 80 to 90 percent of communication is nonverbal. You must pay attention!
- **Look for common interests.** A donor is a person, not a bank account. Part of relating is sharing common life experiences. Maybe that interest is sports or another hobby, or maybe it is some life experience or family challenge.

As you seek to relate to donors, I want to share with you some lessons I've learned from over 25 years of working with donors.

Major donors don't have a lot of people to talk with about their financial situation. This might surprise you, but money can be isolating. When people know you have it, they might treat you differently. A major donor might have an accountant, or a pastor, or a financial consultant, but most donors need an objective advisor with a reasonable level of stewardship expertise who is willing to walk through questions that arise as they seek to be good stewards. Donors need someone willing to ask hard questions and then willing to help them craft a plan and execute that plan. Like Jim in the Fable, you can be that person.

Major donors need a safe place. Talking about money, priorities, and the ramifications of giving large sums of money can feel very vulnerable. As you relate, you may develop a unique relationship where donors share things with you that they won't share with anyone else. In the Fable, Fred and Elisa share vulnerability because of Jim's willingness to build relationships and create a safe environment.

Major donors need impartial advice they can trust. Donors need to know that you are committed to working on their agenda, not only what is best for your organization.

They need to know you are thinking about their resources as assets of God's Kingdom, and you will help them manage those resources, even if that involves giving to multiple organizations. Your common goal is funding the Kingdom and God's larger story!

In line with this idea, major donors need you to be aware and familiar with the environment in which you are asking them to give. This leads me to a few important questions. The answers can affect a donor's mentality and giving. You should know the answer to each of these questions before you meet with a potential donor.

- **Is the stock market up or down?**
    - If stocks are down, the donor may be better off giving some other asset rather than giving stock.
    - If stocks are up, they may have significant appreciation inside their investment portfolio, and it may be more advantageous for them to give stocks rather than to give a cash gift or another asset.

- **Is the economy good or bad?**
    - A strong economy can make your donor feel confident about giving.
    - A bad economy, plagued by fear and volatile markets, can make your donors hesitant to give.
    - The economy also affects taxes on charitable giving and the kinds of gifts that may be advantageous because of how deductions are affected.
- **What is the real estate market like?**
    - If interest rates are low and real estate values are rising, then donors may be more willing to give real estate assets directly to your organization.
    - When the reverse is true and the economy is weakening, stock markets and real estate markets may fall. In this case, the donor may be unwilling to part with a piece of real estate because they're concerned about the valuation.

Relating with your donors is not transactional as much as it is pastoral. Jim's engagement with donors throughout the Fable clearly expresses his care for them as people. He deeply values relationships and engages from the heart. Jim is acting as a steward to stewards. God has called you to shepherd those with resources, and you can't do that without knowing them: knowing them personally, knowing their circumstances, knowing their desires, and knowing the environment affecting their giving. When you really know your donors, you can better advise them about their giving.

CHAPTER 14

EXPLORE

The next step in building an intentional relationship with donors is exploring. Exploring is very closely connected to relating.

As you begin a relationship with a donor, ask engaging questions like:

- How are things going?
- What's happening in your life at the moment?
- What types of issues are you dealing with?
- How's your business?

Keep in mind, as they are answering these questions, you are actively listening and seeking to connect. This isn't an interrogation. You don't want a donor to feel like they are playing 20 Questions.

As you listen to their answers, identify with them.

Don't hijack the conversation. Do respond by sharing a bit about yourself. A relationship with a donor isn't one-sided, so you want to share some of yourself to strengthen the connection.

One of the key components to becoming a better donor development representative, or simply a better relationship builder, is learning to ask good questions. What do I mean by good questions? You want to identify friendly but significant questions that provide meaningful answers. I've found open-ended questions do this best.

An open-ended question leaves room for the person to respond with more than a "yes" or a "no." An open-ended question invites explanation and allows the person to provide more color and more flavor to their answer.

Open-ended questions help build constructive relationships because they reflect an authentic curiosity and tap into the person's basic desire to be known and seen.

As you are asking questions and seeking to relate, you are also intentionally driving the conversation deeper. You have a purpose in meeting with them, and you don't want to lose sight of that purpose. Your questions should seek to reveal your donor's passion and vision for how they want to steward their resources. You are looking for dissonance because you want to identify how you can help them.

Explore questions about significant life changes that might reveal impending opportunities for generosity, solutions you can provide, or examples that reveal your expertise.

The phrase I use the most is "Tell me more." Tell me more about your plans to retire.

Tell me more about your family concerns.

Tell me more about what you are hoping to achieve.

If I could help address some of your concerns, would you be interested in learning more?

When the donor shares something, whether a concern or an opportunity, pivot the conversation toward answers that will help your donor. Much like in the Fable, when April first listens to Mr. Owens' concern regarding supporting missionaries, but then offers the creative solution of a donor advised fund to help him simplify his giving and potentially take advantage of a tax deduction as well.

Now, a word of caution. When you are looking for a particular answer, for example, that a donor is interested in setting up a trust, it is tempting to rush to the finish line. Do not rush to give a quick answer.

When dissonance is revealed, that's when you really begin to explore your donor's situation. If you think you see an opportunity, ask more questions so that you truly understand their situation. You can do more damage than good if you help them into a solution that is not in their best interests.

The exploration step of developing a relationship with donors is a process. It requires time and intentionality. Don't rush it. Ask engaging and exploratory questions, and then ask some more. When you think you finally truly understand the situation, you are ready to Find and Fix.

CHAPTER 15

FIND/FIX

I want to encourage you to expand your role to that of a coach. Like Jim in the Fable, you are the coach of your donors' team. As a coach, you are there to make your donors more effective and to help them be better stewards of the assets God entrusted to them. To be effective, you need some knowledge and to be able to answer their questions, but what makes you a good coach is that you have the trust of your team. They accept and believe in your answers because they know you can help them improve their game.

As a coach, you start with relationships. You move into exploratory questions, and then the next level is creating dissonance. This is where you might find a problem to fix. Donors often have problems they don't even know about or understand. Much like a professional player might have a bad inside-out golf swing or a poor lay-up shot, you can see things they can't.

In the Fable, Jim works through a situation with Roman Crandall. He clearly takes the lead as coach despite the fact that the

Crandalls have outside advisers, and he helps Roman develop a strategy to give more money to charitable causes while also avoiding estate taxes.

Significant transformational gifts of assets, as opposed to a cash gift, often come in the way of fixing a problem rather than a direct ask. Jim didn't ask the Crandalls to give Chrysalis a gift in the form of a Charitable Lead Trust, but he was listening as Roman explained his challenge with his current advisers, and he helped Roman craft the best solution for the family.

As a coach, always begin with the end in mind.

Remember the exit behavior. Before you leave any meeting with a donor, go ahead and set up a call or next meeting to talk about the fix you would recommend. Don't leave a conversation without a clear follow-up plan that you and the donor have agreed upon.

CHAPTER 16

FIX/LEGACY

This approach, seeking to fix problems a donor might not even know they have, might be a different model than you are currently employing. A simple ask for cash, like a gift of $10,000 for a campaign your organization is launching, seems straightforward.

In the story, Jim could have said something like, "Mr. Crandall, can you give us $10,000 for this campaign? You've given us money in the past, you know our vision and mission, and so, will you commit to supporting us as we embark on this new project?"

In some ways, the direct ask is easier and may seem more straightforward. Your organization probably has processes in place to ensure the funds in this campaign go where they need to go. It's a simple ask, but if Jim had chosen that option, he would not have really helped "fix" Roman Candall's problem.

When you move into asset-based giving, you are creating a fix to a real problem your donors face that also may result in a more significant or even a transformational gift to your organization.

Consider the process. Start with engagement. Engagement leads to questions. Questions lead to dissonance. Dissonance creates a problem that the donor might not be aware of, which leads to how your organization can help through an ask or a fix. That's the process we want to follow in engaging the major donor and moving them towards a significant or transformational asset-based gift, as well as what could ultimately be a significant cash gift.

The fix also introduces the idea of legacy, inviting donors to build a legacy that lives beyond a one-time gift. When you think about legacy, whenever possible, you want to engage the entire family so everyone is on the same page. Legacy becomes the impact of their giving and connects donors to the larger story of God's Kingdom.

CHAPTER 17

WHAT DONORS WANT

The donor development process I have outlined is highly relational, built on trust and worthiness developed by you and your organization. Consider the process. Start with relating, which leads to exploratory questions, revealing dissonance. Dissonance creates a problem that the donor might not be aware of, which leads to how your organization can help through an ask or a fix. This is the process we want to use when building intentional relationships with major donors and moving them towards a significant or transformational gift.

Part of the reason relationships are so important is that major donors want more than an opportunity to give to your organization. Honestly, they can find opportunities to give anywhere. What they really want from you is integrated solutions.

As a coach, they need your team to help them strategize a plan that captures their vision and passion and helps them steward their resources holistically in the context of their entire financial life.

Once they have this plan, they need help implementing it. They need someone who helps them steward their assets and achieve their philanthropic goals.

Your organization may or may not offer estate planning, but even if you don't, your team can commit to helping walk with donors through the complex situations that arise in the process of planning. Assign each donor a coach from your team whose role is to ask questions, help the donor think through the ramifications of their choices, gather an inventory of the donor's assets, and seek answers that benefit the donor's specific situation.

The solutions your team provides aren't the only answers. Encourage your team to be honest. When a donor knows they can trust your team to have their best interest at heart, that trust will ultimately benefit your organization.

For example, I was working with a high-net-worth family in California who wanted to give their home to charity.

As we discussed this potential gift, we realized the benefits from giving away their home were offset by the cost of finding a new place to live. I counseled them against making the gift at that time, because it wasn't in the donor's best interest.

However, several years later, when the couple's situation changed, my continued relationship with them allowed me to advise them in the process of giving a significant portion of the proceeds from the sale of their home to charity. Because of my relationship with the donors, the charity ultimately received a seven-figure gift. The donors received a significant tax break because the value of the home exceeded their tax exclusion on a primary residence.

Donor development is all about relationships, and establishing your worthiness means you think about the donor's needs and situation above your own. In the end, donors want your team to be trusted advisors they can lean on to help them reach their philanthropic goals.

CHAPTER 18

CHARITABLE GIFT ARRANGEMENTS

When a donor asks whether they should give via a charitable trust, a gift annuity, or a donor advised fund (DAF), what do you say?

Do you know the difference between these alternatives?

Personal worthiness is about knowing what you can offer as a representative of your organization and what would best meet the needs of the donor.

Like Jim, John, and April, you must know the specifics of each gifting arrangement.

Donors want technical assistance and answers to their questions. You don't need to be an expert in all types of gifts or tax situations, but you need to know where to find the answers a donor needs. This means developing a technical team of experts, people who know the answers to the questions you don't know, people who can help you execute the plan you develop with your donor.

Donors also need you to help synthesize all the information associated with their giving. I used the coaching analogy before, but let's shift a little bit. Think of yourself as a player-coach, someone who can help quarterback the team and manage the many details associated with your donor's giving.

In that role, you need to have a basic understanding of U.S. personal tax law and some of the charitable tools used in estate planning, such as a gift annuity, charitable trust, and donor advised fund. If you aren't familiar with these tools, get familiar with them. Understanding these tools is an important part of advising major donors.

I've worked with many donor development teams, and I have seen many people get intimidated by this part of the job. Don't be. Charitable tax law doesn't change often. You don't need to be a tax expert or an expert in regulatory changes. You just need to know the charitable laws and keep up with the basic elements of how the system works. You need to know the basics of how deductions work and which kinds of gifts minimize state and federal income taxes. You need to know the basics so you can simplify these ideas for donors.

I know it sounds silly, but a partner of mine often uses the illustration of a cow to talk about a charitable trust. I share this with you because this anecdote presents an example of taking a complicated financial strategy and simplifying it so that anyone can understand it.

His illustration looks something like this. A charitable trust is like a cow you own. Because you own it, you want to protect it. When the cow produces milk, it's like the money that comes out of a trust. As long as the cow is healthy and producing milk, everyone is happy. You can divide up the milk: Give some away or designate who gets it. You're not losing anything. The assets in the trust are protected, like the cow safely in your barn, until you die, at which point the charity gets the cow.

This process is relatively simple and easy to wrap your mind around, and the Fable is designed to help address some of the intimidating terminology, like fiduciary, asset allocation, diversification, or investment policy.

CHAPTER 19

THE ASK—CLOSING THE DEAL

You can't engage in a meaningful relationship with donors from the safety of your office. Being intentional with a donor requires regular face-to-face, in-person connections. Throughout the Fable, we see Jim meeting with donors "in person" on a regular basis. Not every meeting with a donor should have an ask, but eventually, you will need to ask the donor for the gift.

When you do, the two keys to asking a major donor for a gift are **preparation** and **presentation:**

Prepare well:

- **Prepare your donor**. Are they expecting to have this discussion? I wouldn't suggest you blindside a donor with a proposal they aren't expecting. Ask "Would you be interested in..." and then follow up on their interest. Now, if they do express interest, you must follow up. Don't let a donor's interest grow cold. Be quick to respond! Your response indicates your personal worthiness and your dedication to the donor and their gift.

- **Know the donor.** How do they want to receive the information? Do they want a spreadsheet and visuals, or is it enough for you to just give a verbal presentation? Do they want numbers or stories about the impact on lives? Do they want time to think about the offer before you meet, or do they need you to walk them through what you are suggesting before you give them anything to think over? Knowing how best to communicate and present is part of what you have been doing as you have built a relationship with the donor.
- **Know the solution you're offering.** Be prepared for the donor's questions. Know why you think this plan or strategy is best for them (not just your organization). Be prepared to walk them through all the ramifications and impact of the gift you are asking them to give.

When it's time to **present**:

- **Read Your Audience.** Are they leaning in or disengaged? How are they coming into the meeting? Is this the best time? Are they really interested in what you have to say?
- **Be Persistent.** Some donors need to talk about a gift over multiple meetings. If they don't say yes right away, don't give up. Ask if they need more information. Ask permission to follow up with them on the idea to see how they feel about it in a few weeks. Until they say no, your job is to keep the conversation going.
- **Practice Clarity and Depth.** This is the hardest one. Different donors have different questions and respond to in-

formation differently. Some donors need lots of details and time. Other donors need to be drawn into a vision and are ready to decide more quickly. You must provide a proposal that appeals to both. Keep it simple, but communicate your "ask" with depth.

- **Flex on 'the fly'.** Even if you do everything right, something may still go wrong. I've seen the email bounce back, the wifi cut out, and a donor representative come down with the flu. You can't plan for every scenario, so be ready to flex on the fly.

Asking a donor for a transformational gift takes practice. You might have already developed proficiency in some of these skills, but you will need to work on others.

CHAPTER 20

DONORS TO CHAMPIONS

As you think about your relationship with the people who give to your organization, it helps to think of how you want those relationships to develop. Consider the example of Jim's relationship with Fred and Elisa Scott. The relationship began with the Scotts attending a golf tournament fundraiser. Their relationship with Chrysalis was initiated by a simple transactional gift.

As you begin your relationship with someone, they will probably be a **donor**, maybe the person who shows up at a fundraising event and writes a check for $100.

You may have many people who give one-time gifts, but the goal is to move the one-time giver into a deeper relationship with both you and the organization so the one-time donor becomes committed to making a recurring gift. When they do this, they become an **investor**. As Jim built the relationship, the Scotts expressed a deeper interest in Chrysalis's vision and mission. They began to "invest" in a more intentional way.

The goal with an investor is to move them deeper in the relationship so that the investor becomes a **partner.** A partner is committed to and aligned with your vision and mission. They are highly focused on the impact your organization can make. Fred and Elisa's deeper engagement and ultimately their trip to Africa with Chrysalis helped grow them into true ministry partners.

Finally, a partner becomes a **champion** when they get others to invest in your organization, too. A champion is passionate about your organization, and they want to provide opportunities for others to be a part of and to invest in your organization. Champions are quick to volunteer, quick to invite others, and quick to share the positive impacts of your organization. A champion might not write a big check, but they give their time and talent as well as their money to support the organization. After multiple trips, Elisa built a true connection with Chrysalis. She became a true Champion. She was excited about the mission and vision and actively shared her stories with those she came in contact with.

Donor development is about creating more committed relationships. Create the context for a donor to understand more about the organization and envision the ways their contribution is making an impact. As your relationship with the donor grows, learn about the donor's vision for their resources, and seek alignment with their vision and your organization.

Turning donors into champions doesn't happen overnight. It's the long game. Our perspective is eternal, and we want to connect our givers to the Kingdom of God through their giving, to be faithful stewards.

SUMMARY

Throughout this book, we have evaluated how we might increase a donor's trust in your organization's worthiness and in your personal worthiness as well. Along the way, I hope you have grown in your own personal worthiness so you can engage more deeply with your donors and build lasting relationships that result in transformational gifts.

In the Introduction to Part Two, I asked you to imagine a world in which your organization is fully funded. I hope you have gathered tools and developed a vision for a new way of doing donor development that will make that fully funded vision possible. As you have seen, earning the trust of your donors isn't complicated, but it does take intentionality, persistence, and action.

At the end of the day, I want you to see the donors you work with. See their passions, their resources, their deep desires, and even their struggles. As you become a steward to stewards, I hope you feel equipped to come alongside them as a trusted advisor, to remind them that stewardship is spiritual, and to inspire them to leverage the great opportunity that accompanies significant resources.

Wealth can be isolating, but you can be an encourager who sees donors giving in an eternal context and who comes alongside donors in meaningful ways.

ABOUT THE AUTHOR

BRYAN TAYLOR is a Principal and the Chief Investment and Executive Officer of Cornerstone Management. Mr. Taylor is a frequent writer and speaker on the global economy and US markets. He has been a conference speaker at Christian Leadership Alliance, Association of Business Administrators Christian Colleges (ABACC), Council for Christian Colleges & Universities (CCCU), Missio Nexus, THINQ, and other Christian nonprofit seminars across the country. He has been serving the Christian nonprofit clients of Cornerstone since 1997.

During his tenure with the firm, Bryan has witnessed the impact of transformational gifts on the charities that Cornerstone serves. He has also enjoyed a unique viewpoint into the lives of donors who became the heroes of giving stories across the faith-based nonprofit universe. In *Worthy of the Gift*, Bryan wields the power of story to bring to life insights he has gained from decades of experience advising both nonprofit leaders and their donors. With expertise in investment consulting, gift and estate design, and corporate management, he is uniquely qualified to illustrate the concept of the worthiness continuum.

www.ingramcontent.com/pod-product-compliance
Lightning Source LLC
LaVergne TN
LVHW051103210926
848486LV00023B/415/J

9781971546063